When a WOMAN Meets JESUS

WHEN A WOMAN MEETS JESUS

MEETS JESUS

Finding the Love Every Woman Longs For

DOROTHY VALCÁRCEL

a division of Baker Publishing Group
Grand Rapids, Michigan

Published by Revell
a division of Baker Publishing Group
P.O. Box 6287, Grand Rapids, MI 49516-6287
www.revellbooks.com

Previously published in 2007 under the title *The Man Who Loved Women* by Winepress Publishing.

Printed in the United States of America

Library of Congress Cataloging-in-Publication Data
Valcarcel, Dorothy.
    [Man who loved women]
    When a woman meets Jesus : New Testament encounters with the Savior / Dorothy Valcarcel.
        p.   cm.
    Originally published: The man who loved women. Enumclaw, WA : Wine-Press Pub., 2007.
    Includes bibliographical references.
    ISBN 978-0-8007-3379-7 (pbk.)
    1. Women in the Bible. 2. Jesus Christ—Friends and associates. I. Title.
BS2445.V35   2009
226′.0922082—dc22   2008055163

Gratitude makes sense of our past,
brings peace for today, and creates
a vision for tomorrow.

Melody Beattie

Dedicated to my parents—
James and Ellen Hardin

. . . for introducing me to Jesus when I was just a child.

. . . for encouraging the thoughtful inquiry and open-minded discussion of spiritual themes as I was growing up.

. . . and for never saying to me, "Dorothy, please stop asking, 'Why.' "

"I've never quit loving you and never will. Expect love, love, and more love!"

Jeremiah 31:3 Message

"Where there is great love there are always miracles."

Willa Cather

Contents

Author's Note

Throughout this book, there are texts of Scripture referenced from several different biblical translations or paraphrases. I specifically used this variety to better clarify the thoughts presented in each chapter.

It is my prayer that you will be refreshed and enlightened as you read these treasures from God's Word.

Unless otherwise indicated, all Scripture references are from the New Century Version of the Bible, copyright © 1987, 1988, 1991, Word Publishing. Other Scripture quotes are from:

AMP	The Amplified Bible
GNT	Good News Translation
KJV	King James Version
TLB	The Living Bible
Message	The Message
NIV	New International Version
NKJV	New King James Version
NRSV	New Revised Standard Version
Phillips	The New Testament in Modern English
RSV	Revised Standard Version

Writer to Reader
with Appreciation

Gratitude is the heart's memory.
French Proverb

I was seven years old when my mother took me to our local library. I had been counting the days until I could get a children's library card and "check out" my first book. The library building was an imposing structure with tall white marble columns, and it was located off the town square on "C" Street. As I walked up the fourteen concrete sculpted steps toward the large front doors, I had a distinct feeling I was entering a thrilling yet undiscovered world.

Awed by the rows and rows of books, my childhood happiness knew no limits. I was certain all the neatly placed volumes, when opened and read, would, as Shakespeare so eloquently penned, give me "the wings wherein we fly to heaven." Little did I know how vast was the wealth at my fingertips.

Whether I read the lyrical poetry of Emily Dickinson, the love sonnets of Shakespeare, the unadorned philosophy of Henry David Thoreau, or the morbid tales penned by Edgar

Allan Poe, books became my hiding place, my secret haven. Books transported me around the world, guided me on exotic adventures, and carried me back in history to times and places I could only daydream about.

My insatiable desire to read motivated me to seek out books on historical events, classical literature, philosophy, and religion. But of all the books I read, one of the most fascinating was the Bible. This book was filled with personal experiences that plumbed the depths of human love and tragedy, and while captivating Bible stories grabbed my attention at first, I found much more contained in that sacred treasure chest. As I studied, I was able to excavate spiritual building blocks that provided a foundation for my life. I was fortunate to have parents and teachers who not only supported but encouraged my study of the Bible, even when it meant I asked difficult questions and, at the same time, demanded answers to some of life's most perplexing problems.

As I grew older and maturity required me to face the decisions and trials of adulthood, I quickly realized that life's critical choices were easier when my "spiritual well" was full. The Bible became the place where I turned to find direction during times of confusion and despair. For when darkness has enveloped me, as it does all of us at one time or another, it has been the well of living water found in the Scriptures that has restored my soul.

At no time in my life was restoration needed more than during a life-changing event that occurred over ten years ago.

Returning home by car from a lengthy business trip, my husband and I were hit head-on by a drunk driver, who died in the accident and nearly took both of us with him. After days on respirators in separate hospitals, my husband and I awoke to lives that had been turned upside down. Following four months in the hospital, as we desperately tried to recuperate from life-threatening internal injuries as well as over thirty-five broken bones each, we were rolled up a ramp into our home, sitting in wheelchairs that were to be our mode of transportation for over a year.

While this catastrophic incident upended our well-laid plans for the future, we found that "in all things God does work for our good" (see Rom. 8:28). Even though I freely admit the severe consequences of this accident have proved to go beyond anything we could ever have imagined, there have also been unexplained joys that have brought immense blessings into our lives.

We met wonderful individuals during our rehabilitation, who labored continually to put our broken bodies back together. The teams of physicians, nurses, physical and occupational therapists gave us the will to try even when we did not have the strength. Our lead rehabilitation physician, Dr. Carolyn Kinney, used not only her medical skill but also her generous heart to inspire and keep us focused on the healing process.

Once we arrived back home, our neighbors Ed and Mattie Monoscalco coordinated a neighborhood catering service. Three days a week, for nearly a year, a van fitted with lifts for carrying two people in wheelchairs arrived to take us to the hospital for an afternoon of outpatient physical therapy. When we returned home at 5:00 p.m., dinner was waiting for us on the counter in our kitchen. Ed constructed wooden ramps that allowed our entire house to become a wheelchair-friendly zone. And along with Wally and Laurie Klein, Ed and Mattie made certain a decorated tree showed up in our house a few days before Christmas. Dr. Angelo Demis, another neighbor, volunteered his time to drive my husband, Jim, to the doctor every day for nearly a month as medical specialists tried desperately to save his right foot from a severe bone infection. Our road to recovery has repeatedly been paved with the love and support of thoughtful family members, kind neighbors, and unselfish friends.

The appreciation my husband and I have for the thousands of prayers, letters, and cards we received during this ordeal is impossible to convey because no words are powerful enough. We especially have deep gratitude for the spiritual encouragement and unfailing prayers of our dear friends, Ivan and Elvera Blake, David and Sharon Kirby, and Mark and Julie Jewett.

Personally, while this time of convalescence forced me to concentrate my energy on physical healing, I also benefited from the solitude that was not possible in previous years because my frantic work pace left little time for reflective thought.

As my recovery progressed slower than planned, I had the opportunity to begin to formulate the outline for this book. Several dear friends stepped forward to assist me in the most extraordinary ways:

Madonna Matheson, whose intuition and astute perceptions have refined this project. Madonna defines the word *friend*.

Pat Privée, whose patience is matched only by her dedication. If you mined Pat's heart, it would be filled with pure gold.

Meredith Simonds, whose unique insights and limitless inspiration are reflected in this book and in the website www .transformationgarden.com.

Brenda Courtemanche, Karen Kehr, and Beverly Ringo, whose attention to detail every day makes the creative endeavors of West Coast Direct Response, Inc., possible.

Betty Carr, who shared her immense creative talent and helped with the artistic development of Transformation Garden. She has been a creative "flint," helping light the fire at just the right moment.

Joe Bodin, who is a master web designer and marketer. My appreciation reflects the gratitude of those individuals around the world who found this book because of his expertise.

Joyce Hart, whose belief and support for this project have been unwavering.

Kathi Macias, whose editorial skills are unparalleled. She understands exactly what it means to "speak a word in season."

And a very special "thank you" to Andrea Doering and the editorial and marketing teams at Baker Publishing Group who generously took a chance on a first-time author.

To family, friends, and individuals I don't yet even know, who visited the website www.transformationgarden.com and offered encouraging words, brilliant ideas, and constructive criticism—all your suggestions have improved this project.

And special "thanks" to Claudia Cucitro at St. Mary's Food Bank, Steve and Carla McRee at Shepherd's Gate, Dottie Phillips, Jan Sitts, Freddie Harris, and Shari Jacobson, who took time to read and provide helpful comments on portions of the manuscript.

I want to express my heartfelt gratitude to Bethanie Johnson, Aimee Murray, Sheryl Parfitt, Ellen Hardin, Mary Olson, Irma Cavanaugh, Jennifer Cavanaugh, Scott and Kathy Cavanaugh, Mae Raines, Rusty Swavely, Adrianne Gambucci, and Hazel Melton, who were not only kind enough to let me use stories about their lives but also allowed the use of their names.

It was Pearl S. Buck who said, "Nothing in life is as good as the marriage of true minds . . . it is life itself." How fortunate I am to be able to share my life with my husband, Jim, my biggest fan, my most trusted ally, and my best friend.

> Yea, gentle voice, though the fair days depart,
> and the skies grow cold above the restless sea,
> God's gifts are measureless, and there shall be
> eternal summer in the grateful heart.
>
> Celia Thaxter, "The Grateful Heart"

I've never quit loving you and never will. Expect love, love, and more love!

Jeremiah 31:3 Message

Where there is great love there are always miracles.

Willa Cather

Bro-ken *(brÿ-ken) adj.*
1. Splintered, fractured, burst.
2. Violated: as, a broken promise.

1

The Broken Women

I am forgotten . . . I have become like broken pottery.

Psalm 31:12 NIV

It was one of the most painful nights of my life. I was sitting by the bed of a close friend who had been brought to the hospital by paramedics who found her unconscious after ingesting a handful of sleeping pills.

As Emma began to regain consciousness, she turned her head in my direction and whispered, "I wish somebody really loved me."

I will never forget those words because I believe they echo a universal longing, the desire we all have to be loved. Not the fantasy love we read about in a fairy tale or the make-believe type of love we see in a movie. Not a romantic flowers and candy love, but an abiding love that lasts forever.

Recently, my twenty-four-year-old niece and I were watching the movie *Ever After* for the fifth time. As the handsome prince rescued his cherished damsel, Bethanie looked at me and sighed, "I wish love happened like this in real life, Effie. But everything doesn't always turn out happily ever after."

I looked at her innocent eyes and beautiful golden hair and thought to myself, *She could have been Cinderella.* Yet even at her young age, she understood the road to lasting love can be bumpy, with potholes and detours along the way.

I know my own pursuit to find the love I dreamed about was not easy. There were times of disappointment and times when my heart ached. In your search for love you may have run into some of the same rocky terrain and been jolted by the rough patches along your way.

One thing I began to realize was that the state of nirvana-like bliss I hungered for always seemed to hinge on finding the right person—the person I thought would be my "true" love. I willingly ignored my own emptiness, hoping someone would come along who would make me feel complete. But just when I thought I had found the perfect person—the one who would unlock the vault to eternal happiness—he would slip away like an elusive butterfly. And I would be left alone, heartbroken and disillusioned.

Often I asked myself, would I ever find what I was searching for? Would the love I longed for be found in the arms of another person? Or would I discover healing for my broken heart in the self-help section of the local bookstore? Sometimes I wondered whether my journey would lead me inside some sacred edifice. Or would my quest finally end with a moment of illumination on a mountaintop?

This book is born out of my personal desire to find a lasting love, a love that would bring me total fulfillment.

I'm talking about the type of love that is there when you go to bed at night and has not left when you get up in the morning. A love that climbs with you to the mountaintop and does not take off when you hit a valley. A love that does not waver when the wind blows in a different direction. A love that turns heaven and earth to find you, then wraps its arms around you and never lets you go. Don't you want to find this kind of love? Doesn't everyone?

If you are searching for a love that fulfills your heart's yearning, I have news for you. You are not alone. You have company; other women who, just like you and me, wanted to be loved, not for who they were or what they were, but simply as they were.

These women came from a variety of backgrounds. They were young and old. Wealthy and poor. Married and single. An unwed teenager and a wealthy socialite. An adulterer and a mother-in-law. An ambitious working woman and a destitute widow. A woman with severe physical disabilities and a woman who could climb any mountain. These women wanted to be accepted, encouraged, and loved, yet all too often they were abused, used, or ignored.

Something in these women's lives was not working, and even though they could not put their finger on the problem, they felt broken. They wanted to get their lives fixed and put back together in working order. As each woman searched—relentlessly—to find what she longed for, her pursuit led to one Man. An ordinary Jewish laborer with a common name—Jesus.

He wasn't a candidate for the current issue of *People Magazine*'s Sexiest Man Alive. He didn't make the Society Register's list of Most Eligible Bachelors. He was not a Harvard graduate. He wasn't handsome or rich. He did not drive a fast car or own a multimillion-dollar home. The establishment detested him. And his job prospects were poor at best.

Yet in spite of a less than promising résumé and a plain appearance, Jesus drew women to his side like a magnet. From his birth to his death they followed him. Long after other people took off in disappoint-

> Women wish to be loved without a why or wherefore; not because they are pretty, or good, or well-bred, or graceful, or intelligent, but because they are themselves.
>
> Henri Frederic Amiel,
> Journal, March 17, 1868

> Man is born broken.
> He lives by mending. The
> grace of God is the glue.
>
> Eugene O'Neill

ment, disgust, or frustration, the women stayed by Jesus's side, hooked like superglue. And I asked myself, "Why?"

I found my answer by examining the way Jesus treated every woman he met.

Instead of pigeonholing women the way society had, he looked at each woman as unique. No one ever heard Jesus trivialize one of their problems by calling it a "woman-thing." He didn't smooth-talk women, or flatter them to get their attention. And he didn't tell them what they wanted to hear—he told them what they needed to know. What's more, he did not believe what many of the women thought about themselves, because so often their own view had been grossly distorted by others. What Jesus did was to focus his attention on each woman's greatest need, and then he met that need—in ways they never expected.

Jesus taught women to look beyond their outward appearance for acceptance. He showed them they were valuable when others said they were worthless. He challenged the rules that bound them and broke down the walls of prejudice that entrapped them. Even when a woman was labeled a "failure," he believed she could be more than her broken past. Most importantly, Jesus gave unconditional love to every woman no matter what her past history, present condition, or future prospects. He was a man ahead of his time, a Renaissance man who understood what loving a woman was all about.

This is why the women stayed with him. And the longer they stayed, the more they grew to love him and to love themselves. When you are accepted just the way you are, encouraged to reach your potential, and empowered to follow your dreams, don't you feel loved?

If you long for a love that restores your self-worth . . . gives you purpose . . . fills you to overflowing . . . and never lets you go, then I invite you to come on a journey with Jesus. Just as he transformed the lives of the women he met, so today, he will transform your life in ways you never imagined.

> He hath sent me to heal the brokenhearted . . . to set at liberty them that are bruised.
>
> Luke 4:18 KJV

A Time for Reflection

> I went down to the potter's house, and I saw him working at the wheel. But the pot he was shaping from the clay was marred in his hands; so the potter formed it into another pot, shaping it as seemed best to him.
>
> Jeremiah 18:3–4 NIV

Exploration

My thoughts on feeling broken . . .

1. Is there a part of my life that is broken?
   Emotionally?
   Spiritually?
   Physically?

2. How long have I felt broken?

3. What have I tried to do to heal my brokenness?

4. What do I believe will heal my brokenness?

5. Has my search for love healed the brokenness I feel?
   How?
   If not, why not?

6. Do I feel loved just as I am—right now?

Inspiration

> Yet, O LORD, you are our Father.
> We are the clay, you are the potter;
> we are all the work of your hand.
>
> Isaiah 64:8 NIV

Recently I decided to take a pottery class at our local art school. Not being what you would call a natural "artist," working at a potter's wheel and learning to mold clay has been a challenge to say the least. More than once, I have found to my dismay, that the small clay pot I was trying to form became a pile of misshapen wet mud. Simply put, my attempt to make something that looked beautiful often turned into an indescribable mess in the hands of an amateur like myself. One evening I pulled the clay off the wheel and headed toward the closest plastic garbage container only to have the professional potter teaching us ask me, "Dorothy, what are you going to do with that clay?"

I thought it was obvious and kept walking. "I'm going to throw it away. It's a lump of wet mud. I can't do anything with it," I whined.

The instructor quickly informed me I was completely mistaken. "Place what you have in that bucket," he said as he pointed to a used can filled with other pieces of clay that looked an awful lot like the unformed lump I was holding. "We'll use it later."

Sure enough, the following week, after his experienced hands had worked the clay into a well-shaped ball, my "mess" became the material I needed to make a lovely small bowl. Trained hands formed something beautiful from the debris I wanted to throw away.

If you have ever felt like my mess of clay, believing nothing beautiful can be formed from the broken shards of your life, take encouragement from the words of the psalmist David: "Your hands made me and formed me" (Ps. 119:73 NIV). Compassionate hands. Experienced hands. Hands that love

20

you and formed you to reflect the beauty the potter sees in you.

> To love is to come to see beyond and despite . . . love sees us as we are, as we really are, and as we can be . . . love sees little but good in us and forgives everything that is not.
>
> Joan Chittister,
> *There Is a Season*

1. What does it mean to be formed by God?

2. Knowing I am formed by God, how does it make me feel?

3. How does this knowledge affect the way I think about myself when I feel broken?

4. What do these words mean to me: "He who made you, who formed you in the womb" (Isa. 44:2 NIV)?

5. In what ways do I believe God can bring healing to the broken places in my life?

[You] will be a vessel for honor, sanctified and useful for the Master, prepared for every good work.

2 Timothy 2:21 NKJV

Affirmations

He heals the brokenhearted and binds up their wounds.

Psalm 147:3 NIV

Daughter, how did you put the jigsaw map of the world together so quickly? Because, Daddy, on the other side was the picture of a man, and when I put the man together, it put the whole world together.[1]

Jack W. Hayford, pastor and author,
Rebuilding the Real You

Flawed *(flÿd)*

n. 1. An imperfection or blemish; defect.

v. 2. To make or become defective.

2

The Flawed Woman

The birth of Jesus Christ happened like this. When Mary was engaged to Joseph, before their marriage, she was discovered to be pregnant.

Matthew 1:18 Phillips

Christmas was a festive holiday around our house. And my childish head was whirling with thoughts of presents wrapped in beautiful paper and tied with fancy ribbons. This particular year I was more excited than usual because my mother and a group of her friends were hostesses for a party at the local community center. After incessant nagging, my best friend and I had worn our mothers down and convinced them to give us permission to tag along to the banquet.

All the ladies planning the party divided up the duties, and my mother was assigned to the decorating committee. It was decided each person in the group would take on the responsibility of decorating one table. This way there would be a variety of tabletops.

A few weeks before the big banquet, my ten-year-old curiosity got the best of me and I began quizzing my mother. "What are you going to do with your table?"

"Well," she said, pausing a moment, "you know I don't have much of a knack for flower arranging, but I'll think of something."

Then she added, "Remember, Dorothy, the goal of the evening isn't to have a fancy table. The idea is to have a great party where people can enjoy the company of their friends."

Several weeks later, our family headed to the community center, leaving home early so my mother could set up her table.

Hours after arriving at the banquet hall, I coaxed my best friend to sneak inside with me to get a close-up peek at the decorations. We wandered up and down the aisles scrutinizing the tables. Some were covered with Christmas greenery. Others were festooned with flowers. And some tables were lit up with glowing candles.

As we came to my friend's mother's table, I gasped and stood transfixed. It was glorious. Magnificent would be the best way to describe it. Laid out on top of a white linen tablecloth were tall crystal candleholders on either side of large poinsettia plants. The velvety red flowers were set off by large white satin bows that sparkled with silver glitter. Sterling silver forks, spoons, and knives were carefully placed next to red napkins held tightly by silver napkin rings. The table stood out. It was by far the most impressive in the hall.

When the goal is "to be perfect" we can thrash around in our flaws and forget about loving others and sharing our gifts with them. We allow the desire to be perfect to oppress us and keep us in the bondage of self-preoccupation. The focus becomes "me" and the effort becomes "trying to perform perfectly."

Adrianne Gambucci,
devotional writer

24

As I walked past the breathtaking array, I looked over at the very next table, and to my dismay recognized everything on it. The plain green vase. The bland tablecloth. The simple napkins lying by stainless steel forks.

It was my mother's table.

How could she bring that ugly vase, I thought to myself. It was an insipid green flat bowl, shaped in a weird form. My mother had laid pansies from our garden in the water, where they floated like life preservers.

As I stood looking at the table, two gossipy women came up behind me. Not knowing who I was from the back, they began criticizing my mother's display. "What a plain table. It's ugly, isn't it?" I wanted to kick both of them in the shins, but I kept my mouth shut and my face forward, hoping they would not recognize me.

Within an hour, the guests began arriving at the banquet hall, and soon all the tables were filled.

I stood by the back door, eyeing the beautiful table with an envious glare. *If only my mother could make her table look like that*, I thought. *Why isn't my mother perfect, like my friend's mom?*

Flawed. Imperfect. Inadequate.

"Funny story," you might say. "Just like a kid. Judging her poor mom on flower décor. Requiring the perfect mother to be an expert at everything, including arranging roses, ferns, and baby's breath."

But before you cast aside the notion this was an incident limited to immature little girls, think for a moment how immature little girls grow up to be mature big girls who often do the same thing. We judge others and ourselves harshly if we are not perfect at everything we do— all of the time. We set our exacting standards so high they are impossible to reach. Then we beat ourselves up when we don't hit the mark.

> Perfection consists not in doing extraordinary things, but in doing ordinary things extraordinarily well.
>
> A. Armauld

I am going to let you eavesdrop on a conversation I had at lunch the other day with a group of longtime girlfriends. It went something like this.

Girl number one: "I had a new neighbor move in next door. I don't like her one bit."

(Laughing)

Girl number two: "What's the problem? Is she nasty?"

Girl number one: "No, the problem is she's nice. Too nice. In fact, she's *perfect*. You know the type. Her house is gorgeous. She's a gourmet cook (already brought me cookies). Her figure's to die for. And her kids are angels."

Girl number three: "Lucky you. Have you thought about moving?"

Girl number one: "No, but let me tell you, I'm just waiting for somebody in my house to say, 'Why can't you be like her?' When they do, they are in for big trouble."

There it was. The "P" word. Rearing its ugly head. Poking its way into our lunch and into our lives.

Perfection. The word that screams out to women, "If only you looked like a Victoria Secret model. If only you cooked like Julia Child. If only you were as good as _____." Go ahead. You fill in the blank.

I know a lot of women who wholeheartedly agree with author Anne Lamott's sentiment, "Perfectionism is the voice of the oppressor, the enemy of the people."

It certainly is the enemy of women. I am a woman. And I have found this enemy is constantly ready to trip me up, causing me to fall into the abyss of self-loathing as I attempt, often unsuccessfully, to live up to my lofty expectations and those of others.

My own ceaseless pursuit to attain perfection gained momentum when I entered high school. Up to that point in my life I had gone to small rural schools, places where it was easy to end up on the top of the heap. There weren't many kids to

26

compete with. But high school presented a new challenge. I attended a big city school and I was a small town girl. All of a sudden I was a little fish in a big pond. I didn't fit in. After much thought I came to the conclusion that the only way to salvage any part of my persistent need to be the best was to try to get the best grades. I could be the perfect student. All the "As" on my report cards attest to the fact I almost accomplished my goal—that is, until I hit Physics. That one class did me in. I still remember the sense of failure I felt when my semester grades came out. There it was. I had gotten a "B."

For days I wept, disappointed in myself. I wasn't perfect anymore. A tough lesson to learn at the age of fifteen—an even tougher lesson if you are forty years old and still comparing yourself to everyone in town. Dissatisfied and unable to enjoy anything you do because it is never quite good enough.

There were a few years when I even resorted to keeping a list of perfection goals. I tried to be the perfect daughter. Tried to be the perfect wife. Tried to be a perfect employee. Tried to keep the perfect house. Tried to be the perfect hostess. I could keep going, but I don't want to bore you. You understand exactly what I am talking about. No doubt you are trying hard, too. You may even have your own list of objectives. Yet, with all our effort, there are always going to be others who are better. Prettier. Thinner. Richer. Smarter. And the casualty in this endless battle is our self-esteem.

Unfortunately, in the war for perfection, nobody wins. It isn't even a draw. There are just a bunch of losers sitting on the sidelines. Some with their noses in the air, others with their heads hung low. Some feeling "better than," others feeling "less than." No wonder the endless toil for perfection has been called "self-abuse of the highest order."

Don't get me wrong. I'm not advocating throwing in the towel and saying, "I don't care how I look or act." That isn't the problem for most women. Instead, the great majority of women I've met are simply worn to a frazzle chasing the gold ring of perfection. As psychologist Dr. Cynthia

Bulick notes, "A perfectionist has really high standards, never meets them, and then beats up on herself for that." If all our sweat and strain were directed at doing our personal best, oblivious to the accomplishments of others, our performance might be worth the effort. But most of the time, the energy we expend is wasted as we enter the comparison game, competing with others for a prime position on the podium of perfection.

Regrettably, the endless struggle to be and do our best seems only to escalate when a woman faces the daunting challenges of motherhood. Maybe it's the result of so-called experts offering their unsolicited judgment, critiquing everything and anything. "Did you see what her kids did? What kind of mother does she think she is? I wouldn't do that if it were my child. I hope she doesn't think she's the perfect mother. Role model? Not her."

This criticism only discourages women who are already strained by their responsibilities. They end up feeling overwhelmed, not by their inability to achieve, but by others' prowess at putting them down.

If you are being punched by an opponent called perfectionism, I'm glad I can tell you—help is on the way.

A messenger has been sent to bring you relief. But I want to warn you, don't be quick to discount the person bringing you assistance. She may not meet your expectations, for she isn't what you or I would call a success. She is not heir to a family fortune. She doesn't have an impressive list of degrees behind her name.

In spite of her apparent limitations, we should pay close attention to her, for she is a bona fide expert on the topic of perfection. That's because she was "selected" to be the mother of a perfect child in an imperfect world. You might think a responsibility this ambitious would require the abilities of a woman with extraordinary skill, amazing insight, incredible talent, unlimited resources, and extensive education. You would have missed by a mile.

If I had been on a committee to choose the best woman to raise a child who would leave an indelible mark on the world, I wouldn't have gotten it right.

Diary of a Flawed Woman

It began like any other day. The sun came up in the east. But it didn't end like any other day, even though the sun still set in the west. By the time this day was over, life for a girl named Mary would never be the same again. This is how Dr. Luke describes the day a teenage peasant girl found out she was going to have a baby:

> God sent the angel Gabriel to Nazareth, a town in Galilee, to a virgin pledged to be married . . . , The angel went to her and said, "Greetings, you are highly favored! The Lord is with you."
>
> Luke 1:26–28 NIV

In one brief moment, this unexpected visitor turned Mary's world upside down.

How would you have responded to news like this? Pregnant. Unmarried. Poor. Untrained.

Mary's response was normal—considering the circumstance surrounding this news.

"Mary was greatly troubled at his words and wondered what kind of greeting this might be" (Luke 1:29).

I find it enlightening to realize that the original Greek translation of the New Testament word *trouble* used by Dr. Luke to describe Mary's reaction really means "to wholly disturb or alarm and agitate."

Mary's whole self, all she was, could not believe what she was told.

Her mind was in a whirl. This must be a dream. More like a nightmare. *What will my parents say? What will my fiancé say? And whose baby is it anyway?*

29

After a few days when reality began to hit, Mary decided a trip out of town for some girl talk was in order. What she needed, as she faced her private predicament, was someone who would not only listen but understand. Just the right person came to mind—her cousin Elizabeth, who was also facing an unexpected pregnancy.

Elizabeth was too old to bear children and had all but given up on having a baby when her husband walked in the door from work one day and dropped this bomb in her lap.

"The baby you wanted is on the way" (see Luke 1:5–25).

Not what you would expect to hear at her age? Within days Elizabeth knew this was no joke. She was going to have a baby. And now, having gotten used to the idea of the patter of little feet, she was visited by her young cousin who came bearing unsettling news of her own.

Elizabeth proved to be sympathetic to the plight of the young, unmarried girl. She gave Mary a shoulder to lean on, a hand to hold, and ears that listened. But if Mary thought this would be everybody else's reaction, she was sadly mistaken.

Arriving back home in Nazareth, Mary was surprised to learn her joy had become fodder for the city gossips. Her "girl next door" image was going to take a beating.

"Did you hear, our little Mary is pregnant? You know the girl down the street. The one we thought was so perfect."

"You don't mean it!"

"Guess what? Joseph, her fiancé, claims the baby isn't his. I hear Mary's been telling people she conceived by the Holy Spirit. What do you think of that tale?"

"I've never heard anything like it. Nobody else in town has used that excuse before. Does she think we'll fall for this crazy story?"

That's very possibly what the neighbors said. It might be what you and I would have said without the pages of history to shed a different perspective on a story that seemed unbelievable.

Poor Mary. Think how she felt as her life was held up for scorn and ridicule. As her reputation was trashed. As her effort to do her best was mocked.

We have a glimpse into her frame of mind during this ordeal when she referred to herself as a woman of "low estate," or what has been translated, "a humiliation." Mary felt that she was the wrong person at the wrong time for the wrong job. If she were "chosen," somebody goofed. She was not old enough, smart enough, rich enough, or educated enough. Sound familiar? Ever heard anybody utter those words before—maybe even to you? "You're just not good enough for this task."

From the outside looking in, it is not difficult to highlight some of Mary's imperfections, beginning with the town she lived in. Not a place where one would be inclined to raise a child like Jesus. It was a small, insignificant town. In John 1:36, one of Jesus's friends, Nathaniel, even went so far as to "cast an aspersion" on the town when he asked, "Can anything good come out of Nazareth?"

And then there was the trip to Jerusalem when Jesus was twelve years old (see Luke 2:41–52). Mary left her child behind in the temple. She forgot him in a crowd. That act alone would have been enough today to file a report with Nazareth's Children's Protective Services. I can just hear the gossip: "Can you believe that inept girl? Forgetting her son. What kind of mother does that? Certainly not a perfect one."

If you were Mary, you would have had a difficult time believing you had done your best if your child wandered the hills with a group of men, was unable to hold down a full-time job, never found a woman to marry, and ended up at parties with drunks and prostitutes. Does a perfect woman raise a boy like that? Was Jesus's unusual behavior the result of good

> If a man is called to be a street sweeper, he should sweep streets even as Michelangelo painted, or Beethoven composed music or Shakespeare wrote poetry. He should sweep streets so well that all the hosts of heaven and earth will pause to say, here lived a great street sweeper who did his job well.
>
> Rev. Dr. Martin Luther King, Jr., civil rights activist and spiritual leader

31

parenting? I don't believe you would have seen Mary's donkey sporting a "tail sticker" proclaiming "I am the mom of a condemned criminal."

If your impression of Mary was that she was the perfect woman raising the perfect child, you may need to reevaluate your belief. The facts tell a different story. She was a poor, uneducated, inexperienced teen, the type of girl I've heard called an "unfit mother."

Had we been privy to Mary's most intimate thoughts—those hidden secrets saved for the pages of her diary—we would not have been treated to the recollections of Nazareth's role model. Nor would we have found a detailed list of Mary's accomplishments. What you and I would have found were the reflections of an imperfect girl. Call it the diary of a flawed woman.

The Man Who Loves Us Just the Way We Are

Jesus entered Mary's life as a baby, an innocent child growing up in a corrupt world. And while history gives us a few glimpses into the relationship between mother and Son, these fleeting glances provide us with a limited picture.

By all accounts, Mary's story about the heritage of her child was a dubious one. To make matters more difficult, she was attempting to raise her child in a town with a reputation for producing losers. With this background, we might expect that as Jesus grew, he would disassociate himself from his past, even from his family. There were facts in his background he might want to omit from his résumé. When out with friends, he might want to embellish his genealogy—focus on the King David lineage, not the unwed mother bloodline.

But he didn't. Whether he was at a wedding assisting his mother when the wine ran out or visiting his family in Nazareth or teaching on a mountainside with his brothers at his side, Jesus chose to embrace his history as well as the woman he called "Mother." Why? Because this loving Man recognized that his mother, though flawed, had given him the best she had to give. Even if other people thought Mary had nothing to offer, Jesus loved her because she had everything to give. She never held back her best from him. And I ask you, what more can we do than give our best?

This is why the Son honored his mother. But what's more, Jesus knew that nothing gives a woman more satisfaction than to receive the approval of the object of her affection. And this was what Mary needed from her Son. She needed his affirmation. She needed to know he thought she had done her best.

Isn't that what every woman wants? Don't you want to know the person you love thinks you've done your best? Even if you are flawed and faulty, weak and failing.

So at the time of Mary's greatest need, when she was losing the Son she loved, Jesus made certain his mother was given the validation she deserved. He honored her in a way that reverberates with every woman who is trying to be her best. As he hung on a Roman cross between two thieves on a hill called Golgotha, Jesus turned to his most loving friend, John, and asked him to care for his mother. This was a touching reminder to this woman that he loved her and would never forget what she had done for him. At that moment, Jesus sent a message to the world that even if some thought Mary was a girl of low station, her son recognized she was a woman with a high calling.

Let there be no doubt. The woman everybody thought was all wrong was all right for Jesus. Not because of what she had or how she looked, but because of what she gave him: encouragement, strength, courage, and love. Qualities every woman carries within herself. Qualities every woman has to give. This is why Jesus's mother, Mary—as imperfect as she might appear on the surface—is the perfect woman to carry a message to you and me. This young teenager gave herself totally to a heavenly task. In Mary's own words, "Behold, I am the handmaiden of the Lord; let it be done to me according to what you have said" (Luke 1:38 AMP). Jesus's flawed mother brings us the good news—when you give your whole self you are giving your best and that's perfect!

Our Need—His Response

If you feel like you are still falling short of your expectations, if a voice continues to whisper in your ear, "You're not good enough," then you need to pay attention to the message Jesus has for you. It's a message of relief to a woman who is trying with all her might to be the best she can be.

Aren't you thankful the woman chosen to be Jesus's mother was an imperfect woman like you and me? Not some girl who was worth a million dollars and never had to work a day in her life. Not a mother with one child and two nannies. Not a woman who had never known poverty and heartache, or ridicule and scorn.

Mary's life demonstrates in a dramatic fashion that heavenly choices often look far from perfect to earthly eyes.

Just take my own childish view of my mother. Remember, she's the one whose banquet table was a decoration wasteland. Well, guess what? By the end of the evening, when I believed her guests would be appalled by her lack of creative ability, I noticed something strange going on at my mom's table. I watched as her guests laughed and talked, completely absorbed in the fun of time well spent with friends, oblivious to the lack of flower décor. And where was my mother? She was the one person who never sat down all evening. Instead she became a human ferry, taking food from the buffet table to her guests. They never wanted for a thing—mother made certain of that. She may not have had the most beautiful table, but if you had asked her guests, they would have said she had the best table. And guess what, through the years, on many occasions my mother and I have combined our talents—she cooks and I decorate—and you know something? By sharing the best of our abilities with each other, we make a "perfect" combination.

I invite you to take a look in the mirror. The person staring back at you—the woman who is always trying so hard to measure up, the woman who is trying to be perfect—may be a Mary. Young. Inexperienced. Uneducated. Poor. Unmarried. Pregnant. Yet in spite of your imperfections, you are the Son's choice for a task fitted perfectly for your skills. All he asks you to do is give your best. That's what Mary did—and that's why she was perfect. The same goes for you.

> Yes, mother . . . I can see you are flawed. You have not hidden it. That is your greatest gift to me.

> Alice Walker, *Possessing the Secret of Joy*

A Time for Reflection

The Flawed Woman: Mary, Jesus's Mother
Background Texts: Matthew 1:16, 20; 2:11; 13:55; Mark
  6:3; Luke Chapters 1 and 2; Acts 1:14

Exploration

My thoughts on perfection . . .

1. How do I define the word *perfect*?

2. Based on my definition of perfection, I find myself aspiring to be perfect in what area(s) of my life? Why? In what area(s) of my life have I achieved, or at least come close to achieving, what I believe to be "perfection"?

3. In what area(s) of my life do I feel I have failed the most?

4. How does this affect the way I think about myself?

5. What qualities would I include on a list describing the "perfect" woman?

6. What qualities would I include on a list describing the "perfect" mother?

Inspiration

"Imperfection is the crack in the armor, the 'wound' that lets God in." As Meister Eckhart wrote in *The Spirituality of Imperfection* almost seven hundred years ago: "To get at the core of God at His greatest, one must first get into the core of himself [herself] at his [her] least."

1. After getting acquainted with Mary, in what ways has my view of perfection changed?

2. What qualities made Mary a perfect mother?

3. What do the biblical words in Matthew 5:48, "Be ye perfect," mean to me?

Perfection

> To be perfect
> Even as your Father in Heaven is perfect . . .
>
> How, O God, am I to understand the word?
> Perfect and pure in heart?
> What means pure?
> Pure, pure, pure apple juice!
> I begin to sense a clue.
> Pure apple juice is made from the whole apple;
> bruises, blemish, skin, core—the whole imperfect works.
> Pure apple juice is not pasteurized, refined, filtered,
>   nonentity!
> Bruises, blemishes, skin and core.
>
> To be perfect is to be whole, a paradox
> even as our Father in Heaven.[1]

> Mary Caroline Richards, poet,
> *Laughter, Silence, Shouting*

36

Jesus's relationship with Mary teaches us three lessons about perfection.

1. I am not perfect because of what I have. I am perfect because of what he gives.

> For even the Son of Man did not come to be served, but to serve, and to give his life as a ransom for many.
>
> Mark 10:45 NIV

How can I serve?

2. I am not perfect because of what I do. I am perfect because of what he does.

> Finish what you started in me, God. Your love is eternal—don't quit on me now.
>
> Psalm 138:8 Message

What area of my life do I want God to keep working on?

3. I am not perfect because of who I am. I am perfect because of who he is.

> I am the light of the world. Whoever follows me will never walk in darkness, but will have the light of life.
>
> John 8:12 NIV

How can his light shine through me?

> For the eyes of the LORD run to and fro throughout the whole earth, to shew himself strong in the behalf of them whose heart is perfect toward him.
>
> 2 Chronicles 16:9 KJV

Affirmation

> God is always on the alert, constantly on the lookout for people who are totally committed to him.
>
> 2 Chronicles 16:9 Message

Empty *(imp'ti)* adj.
1. Containing nothing.
2. Lacking substance; meaningless.

3

The Empty Woman

There was also present, Anna, the daughter of Phanuel of the tribe of Asher . . . she was a very old woman, having had seven years' married life, and was now a widow of eighty-four years.

Luke 2:36–38 Phillips

It was a long walk from the car to the apartment where my husband, Jim, was waiting after coming home from work. The news I was carrying made the distance seem even farther.

"How was your visit to the doctor?"

It didn't take but a few seconds for Jim to realize by the look on my face that this had not been a routine office visit.

"The doctor said he has to do more tests, but he doesn't think I'll ever be able to have children."

The words hung in the air with no place to go. Bad news is never easy to hide.

"Maybe he was wrong," Jim said in a hopeful tone. "Let's wait and see what happens. We'll get another opinion."

And we did. Doctor after doctor. Test after test. Then it came. The verdict was final. I would never be able to bear children.

At the time, Jim and I were young and had a lot on our plates, so the initial shock of our situation numbed us to the long-term reality that we might be childless.

But as time passed and family members and friends had children, we began to feel something was missing in our lives. Over the next five years we made inquiries into the possibility of adoption. Unfortunately, every time we were told we were next in line for a baby, "our child" would end up in another home. Time after time we would get close to having a baby in our family, only to see our hopes dashed. Disappointment surrounded us like a dark cloud.

After one particularly heart-wrenching experience, our doctor suggested we attend a support group designed specifically to assist infertile couples with the challenges of not only their medical situation, but also the social results of not conceiving a child.

I will never forget leaving the first meeting. It was depressing, to put it bluntly. Many of the people in the room had been devastated by the news they would not have a child of "their own." As we left the group at the end of an emotional evening, I vowed to myself that no matter what the future held, I did not want to live the rest of my life feeling so desolate. There had to be something—someone to fill my empty arms and ease the ache in my heart.

Empty. Barren. Vacant.

Is there something missing in your life? Do you have a vacant spot in your heart? A place that is unfilled?

For my mother that empty spot was left when her husband, my father, died suddenly. In one moment she lost her best friend, a friend she had shared her life with from the time she was eight years old. Since my dad's death twenty years ago, there has been a void in Mother's life. There is a vacant chair at the dining room table. There is a cold space in her bed. And worst of all there is an empty spot in her heart.

> May we never let the things we can't have, or don't have, spoil our enjoyment of the things we do have and can have.
>
> Richard L. Evans

For my sister, the empty spot came several years ago when her younger child went off to college. There is a name for what she is experiencing. We call it the "empty-nest" syndrome.

"It sure is quiet in the house," she confided to me. "I never realized I could feel so alone. With Aimee and Bethanie gone, the house is like a vacant lot." You may be able to relate to her situation if your children have left home.

Possibly there are other reasons you feel empty. A spouse may have left you for another person, someone younger or prettier. And now the hole in your heart is filled with a pain that seems to increase by the day.

Or perhaps you have a child who has run away from home or gotten caught up in the clutches of drug addiction. Every day you worry and wonder. But most of all you ache, fearing the next phone call may be the last. And your empty feeling is only made worse by the memory of days, not so long ago, when there wasn't an empty chair at the breakfast table or an empty room in your house.

It could be that like myself and nearly 10 million other women in the United States you are unable to have the child you dreamed about. You have tried everything, gone to every doctor, tried every medication, had every surgery, and finally you have been forced to live with the fact you will not conceive. Now, you are left with empty arms that echo the emptiness in your heart.

If you are missing something and a vacancy sign hangs over the door of your life, then you need to get acquainted with the woman who helped me realize there is a cure for those of us who face living "barren" lives. The lady's name is Anna. From morning to night, for over seventy years, she stared the problem of emptiness in the face.

The Empty-Nest Poster Girl

In order to understand Anna, we must take a step back in time. At first glance, with only three texts in the entire Bible mentioning her name, it is easy to surmise that Anna's story isn't even worth our trouble to talk about. Wrong!

Even though there isn't a lot of space in Scripture given to Anna's encounter with Jesus, there is more to their relationship than first meets the eye.

Let's begin by looking at what we know about this godly woman:

1. Anna was a prophetess. The Greek translation calls her an "inspired" woman. In the Old Testament, Miriam, Moses's sister (Exod. 15:20), Deborah (Judg. 4:4), and Huldah (2 Chron. 34:22) were all women who, in the Hebrew language, were called "prophetess." Some historians refer to these women as "wives of prophets." Other biblical scholars believe Anna may have been the wife of a priest. In our time we might call her "the pastor's wife." But one thing all these women had in common was that they were held in high regard because of their spiritual leadership, not only in their own homes but by others in their community.

2. Anna was the daughter of Phanuel, of the tribe of Asher. Years before Anna was even born, the entire tribe of Asher had been taken captive by the Assyrians, and as a group, they never officially returned to the Promised Land, Israel. However, since Anna was in Jerusalem at the time we meet her, it is obvious someone in her family, most likely a male family member, remembered their family's roots and either returned with their

> Abundance is, in large part, an attitude.
>
> Sue Patton Thoele, *The Women's Book of Confidence*

loved ones to the land of their birth or arranged for Anna to marry a man in Jerusalem who reflected the spiritual values her family treasured.

3. Anna was married for seven years and had not borne a child when her husband died. To understand the situation she found herself in, one has to look no further than Old and New Testament history to realize that being a childless widow was an undesirable plight. When women bore children, they were called "blessed." But if they did not get pregnant, people assumed a "curse" of God was upon them. Husbands could, as Genesis 16:1–6 tells us Abraham did, take another woman to be the mother of their children. And I might add, the Bible lets us in on the sordid details of Abraham's paternity plight with Sarah and Hagar. What a mess this situation turned out to be for all parties involved.

> All the great blessings of my life are present in my thoughts today.
>
> Phoebe Cory, *My Blessings*

Later in the book of 1 Samuel, chapter 1, the story is told of Hannah, who is described as "embarrassed and grieving" because the Lord had left her childless. To compound her troubles, even though her husband, Elkanah, loved her dearly, he married someone else who gave him children, and the rival wife "taunted Hannah cruelly, rubbing it in and never letting her forget that God had not given her children" (1 Sam. 1:6 Message). Hannah's distress became so severe that one year, when she went to pray at the temple, Eli the priest witnessed Hannah talking to herself, concluded she was drunk, and told her to "Sober up!" (1 Sam. 1:14 Message). The tragic picture painted in the story of Hannah gives only a glimpse into the lives of childless women. King Solomon went farther when he described a sterile woman in a most derogatory manner: "There are three things that are never satisfied, four that never say, 'Enough!': the grave, the barren womb, land, which is never satisfied with water, and fire, which never says, 'Enough!'" (Prov. 30:15–16 NIV). Quite a way to talk about women, who through no fault of their own find themselves unable to bear the children they long to have. When a woman is branded an undesirable commodity, what man would want to marry someone who could not give him an "inheritance"? To put it bluntly, Anna's marriage prospects were poor at best.

4. Anna became a widow at a young age. Since most women in New Testament times married at thirteen or fourteen years of age, Anna was not much more than twenty when her husband died. Luke states she had not left the temple since her husband's death, so it is quite likely she found herself in tight financial straits, which was the condition of most widows in biblical history. The tough times faced by a woman with no husband to support her were legendary in those days. Over twenty times the Bible requires that special care be shown to widows. And in the New Testament, widows are singled out as worthy of merciful care.

So here is Anna's situation. With no future marriage plans and no children, the world she faced looked bleak indeed. Hers could easily have become a life underscored by what she did not have, a life mapped out by what was missing. A life defined by emptiness. But to think this would be Anna's fate would mean you and I did not know her very well. For rather than hide under the covers and boohoo about her plight all day long, whimpering, "Poor me. I don't have a husband. I can't have a baby. What am I going to do?" Anna chose to follow a different path.

She made the decision not to wallow in the valley of lack, but to climb to the peak of plenty. And it was on this mountaintop that she found the place where abundance resides. You might say Anna struck it rich when she staked her claim to the bounty waiting for those individuals living expectant lives. Anna never focused her attention on what she didn't have. Instead she kept

> The joy of a spirit is the measure of its power.
>
> Ninon de Lenclos

44

her life open to receiving what she was promised. And how did she accomplish this incredible task? Anna embraced the joy of others and allowed it to become her own.

In order to have her dream fulfilled, Anna knew she must be where there were people who needed her. So she planted herself in the center of the busiest spot in town, the local temple, the hub of Jewish life. It was here where children were brought at birth to be blessed; it was where young people were taught; it was where couples married; it was where town worshipers convened; it was where public decision making took place; and it was where people came for solace in times of trouble. The temple was the focal point of the community. But for Anna it became the focal point of her life. It became the place where she concerned herself with the needs of others rather than sitting alone at home to mope about how rough her life was.

For eighty-four years the Bible says Anna "departed not from the temple, but served God with fastings and prayers night and day" (Luke 2:37 KJV). This is a record for days on the job. Soon everyone in town recognized her. This quiet woman moved among temple visitors, held other people's babies, laughed with other people's children, prayed for other people's families. As generation after generation came to the temple, they were encouraged by a faithful woman who lifted the load of those who needed her smile, her joy, and, yes, her love. No bitterness for what she was not given, just praise for how much she had.

Yet all the while, Anna kept praying that soon the one baby she longed to see would be laid in her outstretched arms. And just when she thought her time might run out, guess what? Anna got the surprise of her life.

The Man Who Fills You to Overflowing

For Anna it started out like any other workday. She went to the temple. And like other days, there was a bustle of

45

activity, a continuous flow of foot traffic. No one paid any attention to the poor young couple who entered carrying two turtledoves—one of the least expensive offerings anyone could present at the temple service. They were just a blur in the hundreds of faces in a nameless crowd. But long ago Anna had made a conscious decision to pay attention to each person she met. She looked at each face. She cared about every heart. That is what you do when you are waiting for your empty arms to be filled with a promised gift. Every individual becomes important. And on this particular day, Anna was watching. She wasn't just passing time at her job, waiting to move into a retirement home for worn-out prophetesses. She wasn't thinking about a vacation day on the shores of Galilee. She had work to do, and as long as she was able, she would stay on duty and keep her arms open to others. You see, Anna didn't just happen to be in the right place at the right time, she chose to be there.

No wonder the young couple was drawn to her side. No wonder they wanted to lay their baby in her empty arms. No wonder an old woman was filled to overflowing. And no wonder an outburst of unbridled jubilation was heard coming from Anna's lips. When your empty arms are filled and your heart is spilling over with joy, it is impossible to keep silent.

With exuberance, Anna's voice was heard throughout the temple as she "returned thanks to God" (Luke 2:38 AMP). At over one hundred years of age, Anna finally was filled to overflowing with the gift she had waited for all her life. Jesus made certain of that. He came into Anna's life and met the need of her heart at just the right time and in just the right way.

Our Need—His Response

Like Anna, are you waiting to have that empty spot in your life filled?

46

Have you been suffering quietly—and alone—waiting and hoping that someday the vacancy sign in your life will say, "Standing Room Only"?

If you fear you will never have that empty spot in your heart filled, I ask you to remember Anna, and remember what Jesus did to meet the need in her life and fill the longing in her heart. You see, in order to take away Anna's emptiness, Jesus had to come to her in a unique way. Not as a teenage boy, like he did when he met the learned scholars in the temple. Not as a prophet, like he did when he cleansed the temple. Instead, Jesus came into Anna's life when he was a helpless infant. For Anna it was the only gift she had prayed for her entire life. And that is why coming to her as a baby was the only way Jesus could answer her prayer. All I can say about the lengths Jesus goes to to meet our needs is, "WOW!"

Anna never gave up looking and serving and praying—and heaven watched, and at the perfect moment her empty heart was filled to overflowing, as the baby she had longed for since she was a young bride was laid in her outstretched arms.

If you are waiting for someone to fill that empty spot in your life, keep your eyes open wide and your arms outstretched. For just when you think life has passed you by, like Anna, Jesus will give you the someone who fills your emptiness.

Believe me, I know firsthand, the barren life you think you may face will be filled to overflowing when you least expect it. I have had my own empty arms filled by nieces and nephews, foster children, and even strangers who needed a caring aunt or an understanding friend or a shoulder to cry on. They needed a person just like me, who was not too busy with her own children, so she had time and energy to give them the love they needed—at the right moment.

Several weeks ago, my niece Aimee and her husband, Ben, flew home from Dallas where they live. The reason for their visit was a special occasion—the dedication of their new baby girl, Elise Nicole. In the presence of family and friends, these young parents made a commitment to raise their child with the same spiritual values they had been taught as children.

As our family surrounded them, I felt a few tears roll down my cheeks, when I recalled a similar event twenty-four years earlier, the day my niece, Aimee, was dedicated. How thankful I was that over the years I was able to be involved in her life as she grew into a beautiful, spiritual woman. That afternoon at dinner, Aimee came to me and said, "Effie, it was so important this day happened at this time because the dress Elise wore today was the same one you got for me to wear at my dedication, and now my baby wore the dress too."

Later as I cradled little Elise in my arms, I was again reminded that when your arms are filled and your heart is overflowing with joy, it is impossible to feel empty.

Like Anna, keep your arms open wide. You may have waited a long time—maybe even eighty-four years. Yet who knows? Today could be the day Jesus will fill you to overflowing and the barren spot in your life will become fertile again. "He gives childless couples a family, gives them joy as the parents of children. Hallelujah!" (Ps. 113:9 Message).

> Our mouths were filled with laughter,
>   our tongues with songs of joy.
> Then it was said . . .
>   "The LORD has
> done great things for [her]."
>
> Psalm 126:2 NIV

> "He settles the barren woman in her home
>   as a happy mother of children.
> Praise the LORD."
>
> Psalm 113:9 NIV

A Time for Reflection

The Empty Woman: Anna, the Prophetess
Background Text: Luke 2:36–38

Exploration

My thoughts on feeling empty . . .

1. What event in my life has left me feeling empty?

2. How did this event affect my life?

3. What have I tried to do to feel "filled up" again?

4. What have been the results of my effort?

> Emptiness is a gift that opens us further to the trans-forming power of God.
>
> Adrianne Gambucci, devotional writer

Inspiration

I credit my high school English teacher with the brilliance to instill in me a great love of poetry. She inspired our entire class by reading poetry. But she also encouraged us to spend time reading the works of great poets outside of school.

One of the first poems I learned was by the English poet William Wordsworth, which begins, "I wandered lonely as a cloud." I call this an "Ode to the Daffodil." It is a poem that in the most rapturous words captures the beauty of bobbing daffodils filling a field with their golden glory. From the first time I read this poem as a young girl, I wanted to run down to the local nursery, buy some daffodil bulbs, plant them, and wait for spring when they erupted from the earth.

Over the last several years, I have had a young neighbor help me plant daffodil bulbs around my yard. I thought I could remember exactly where all the bulbs were hidden, but to my surprise and delight, bulbs are popping up everywhere. Places I'd thought were barren spots of dirt have yielded multiple leaves of green and flowers of vibrant yellow hue. Winter, in all its cold desolation, has been replaced by dynamic life.

Hidden from my view over the last few months, nature has been at work. Nutrients planted in the earth have joined with water to feed this floral array that adorns the slope on the hill behind our house.

Beauty was flourishing even though I couldn't see it. Barren land has been replaced by blooming bulbs.

In his thought-provoking book, *Waiting*, Ben Patterson observes:

> God is for you, not against you; He feels your ache, He hears your groaning. And note: If He is silent now . . . it is the silence of His higher thoughts. He is up to something so big and so unimaginably good that your mind cannot contain it . . . what we see God doing is never as good as what we don't see.[1]

Feeling empty today? Something has been planted in your life. And God is providing you with the nutrients of his love and the water of his grace. Spring is right around the corner. I can hardly wait to see what will bloom.

> Wilderness and desert will sing joyously, the badlands will celebrate and flower—like the crocus in spring, bursting into blossom, a symphony of song and color.
>
> Isaiah 35:1–2 Message

1. What lessons have I learned from Anna's solution to the emptiness in her life?

2. What can I do that would make it possible for me to wait as long as Anna did to have my empty arms filled?

3. How and for whom can I extend my open arms and loving heart?

4. What empty place in my life would I like to have God fill?

> To complain that life has no joy while there is a single creature whom we can relieve by our bounty, assist by our counsels or enliven by our presence, is to lament the loss of that which we possess, and is just as rational as to die of thirst with the cup in our hands.
>
> Thomas Fitzosborne

Affirmations

> Be glad and celebrate! God has
> Done great things . . . The fields and
> Meadows are greening up.
> The trees are bearing fruit again.
>
> Joel 2:22–23 Message

More is being planned for you by God than had been prayed for by us.

> S. D. Gordon

Reject *(ri-jekt)* v.

1. To refuse to accept, submit to, believe, or make use of.

2. To refuse to consider or grant; deny.

3. To discard as defective or useless.

4

The Rejected Woman

In Samaria he came to a town named Sychar, which was not
far from the field that Jacob had given to his son Joseph.
Jacob's well was there, and Jesus, tired out by the trip, sat
down by the well. It was about noon. A Samaritan woman
came to draw some water, and Jesus said to her, "Give me
a drink of water." (His disciples had gone into town to buy
food.) The woman answered, "You are a Jew, and I am a
Samaritan—so how can you ask me for a drink?" (Jews will
not use the same cups and bowls that Samaritans use.)

John 4:5–9 GNT

My father was six months old when his mother died
suddenly.

Unable to keep the family together, my dad's father left his
young baby in the care of a neighbor in Arizona while he returned to Tennessee where, with the help of family members,
he hoped eventually to reunite his children. But his plan did not
materialize, and it wasn't long before he became ill and passed
away, leaving children scattered across the United States.

53

Without a mother or father, my dad continued to live in the neighbor's home, separated from a family he was too young to know existed. As Daddy grew older, little was mentioned about his past. When any of his brothers or sisters tried to visit him, they were told, "Jimmy doesn't want to see you." And when my dad asked about his family, he was told they didn't want him. He had been given away.

It was a traumatic beginning for a young life. Times were tough. Money was tight. The house where my dad lived was small and cramped. As soon as he was old enough, his bed was put outside on a drafty screen porch to make more room inside the house. Wintertime found my dad frequently ill with pneumonia. The repeated infections resulted in long-term health problems that challenged him most of his adult life.

By the time Daddy was a teenager, he had lost contact with most of his brothers and sisters and started using the name of the people he lived with. It stopped the teasing by kids at school who were curious as to what happened to his "real family."

As Daddy shared with me years later, "There were days when I would walk home from school and stop behind an old broken down barn not far from where I lived. I would sit on the ground where no one could see me, and cry. I would ask myself over and over, 'Why do I have to be the boy without a mom and dad? Why doesn't somebody love me?'"

Then sadness came over his face as he reflected on the days in his past. "Life was difficult then, because all I wanted to know was that I belonged to someone."

He grew up believing he was not wanted, thinking no one cared about him, feeling he did not belong to anyone.

> Sometimes at that moment [in despair] a wave of light breaks into our darkness, and it is as though a voice were saying: "You are accepted. [You are accepted,] accepted by that which is greater than you."
>
> Paul Tillich, *The Shaking of the Foundations*

Rejected. Cast-Off. Shunned.

"You don't belong to me." "I don't want you anymore." "You aren't part of our family." "I wish I had never had you."

Have you ever heard these words? Has someone told you they wished they could get rid of you? Are you a rejected child? A rejected girlfriend? A rejected wife? A rejected mother?

Have you been left feeling as though nobody wants you? That you don't belong to anyone? That if you dropped dead today, no one would care?

Unwanted. It's a cold word. Yet how easily it slips off our tongues. Unwanted pregnancy. Unwanted child. Unwanted nuisance. It makes you feel like a heavy choke chain hanging around somebody's neck, an annoyance that clutters someone's life.

Unwanted. A feeling caused by the rejection we experience when a parent walks out on us, leaving us with a lifetime of lost memories. Or the painful sense we feel when harsh words are hurled our way. Or the abandonment that results when some secret is uncovered.

Several years ago, a close friend confided she had just found out she had been adopted. "I love my parents; don't get me wrong. But, I know there will always be a part of me that wonders why somebody would want to give me away," she confessed with absolute candor.

Rejection takes a toll on our ability to feel like we belong. But worse yet, rejection can rob us of our self-worth.

No one could better assess the damage done by rejection than Mother Teresa, whose orphanage served as a safety-zone for India's cast-off children. After seeing the devastation caused in the lives of youngsters who were left homeless, she noted, "The worst illness today is not leprosy or tuberculosis, but the sense of being unwanted, of not being loved, of being abandoned."

If, like my father, you feel as though you don't belong to anyone—if you have felt the sting of rejection—then come take a walk with me to the well in a city called Sychar. There a lonely figure approaches. She is carrying an empty pot on her head. If you look closely, you will see she has a tear in her eye. It is caused by the hole in her heart. And her pain is the result of the realization she is not wanted.

No Place to Call Her Home

This Samaritan girl's life could be the blueprint for a country song entitled "You Aren't Wanted Here Anymore."

First, she was born into a culture filled with dissention. Believe me when I say that she wasn't the one who started the quarreling between the Jews and Samaritans. Even though these two groups were really family, all descendants of Abraham, they did not get along. And during Jesus's life, one of their greatest points of contention was the location of a temple to worship God.

The Samaritans lived in a region called Samaria. Settled by their ancestors who were from the bloodline of the ten northern tribes of Israel, these tribes had decided years before that it was too far to travel to Jerusalem to worship, so they built their own temple on Mount Gerizim. This was a slap in the face to Jewish worshipers who believed Jerusalem to be not only the chosen geographical location but also the God-ordained site for the temple. What made the relationship of these two groups even more contentious was activity documented by Jewish historian Josephus, who described how the Samaritans turned into fair-weather relatives. At times when foreign armies attacked both groups, the Samaritans chose to throw their support behind the nation they perceived would help them the most, even when it was a foreign country that could do harm to their family members in Galilee and Judea. Of course, this infuriated the Jews, who felt a unified front would be a better way to conquer an enemy.[1]

Into this environment a baby was born. A Samaritan. But that wasn't the biggest problem. What was worse, this baby was a girl. And to be a woman at this time in history put you on a level not much better than an animal.

When this young girl married she never imagined the trouble she was going to face. If she thought marriage was forever, she was wrong. And there was good reason to be worried if you were a woman entering into a "marriage arrangement" over two thousand years ago. Women were considered property, first owned by their fathers, then by their husbands. No time for dating. No choice as to whom you would like to spend your life with. Marriage was a business deal between a willing father and an appropriate male. Once the marriage papers were signed and sealed, your husband, the new owner, had all rights over his property.

Watch out girls! If you burned your husband's dinner, lost one of his sheep, or didn't make love to his satisfaction, down to the local elders he would go—another all-male committee—tell them what he didn't like about you, say three times, "I divorce you," and send you back home to Dad. That easy. That quickly. That harshly.

So what happened to the poor Samaritan girl? Well, the first thing you know, husband number one said he did not want her anymore. When husband number two said, "Move on down the road," she was not quite as surprised. By the time husband number five sent her packing, she was already walking, right into the arms of number six. This time, though, she did not bother getting married. She had found out nothing lasts forever, so why inconvenience herself or anybody else by putting her clothes in the dresser or her toothbrush in the medicine cabinet. She had given up looking for a place to hang her hat, for a place she could call home.

Hopefully, if she was good at the chores, man number six would keep her around for a

> The body is a house of
> many windows, there we
> all sit, showing ourselves
> and crying on the passerby
> to come and love us.
>
> Robert Lewis Stevenson

while. So she did her work without complaint, even if it meant lugging heavy pots back and forth to the well every day.

If only she could get the water in the early morning or late evening like all the other women. But don't kid yourself; the fine ladies in town wanted no part of her. And they certainly didn't want her around their husbands and children. So she was forced to suffer the heat of a noonday desert sun beating down on her head. The penetrating rays served as a constant reminder that she did not fit in with the crowd. Maybe it was better this way. She couldn't take the finger-pointing . . . the whispering . . . and those ugly stares. She was an expert at knowing when and where she didn't belong. And in this town there wasn't a welcome mat out for her. She was an outsider in an insider's world.

The women in town had enough of her—the men had too much of her. Like yesterday's garbage she had been tossed out on the scrap heap of life. She was unclaimed refuse that did not belong to anyone.

The Man Who Loves All His Children

As the woman approached the well she saw a man, a Jewish man who asked her for a favor.

"Will you please draw me a drink of water?"

She was stunned. This guy has got to be joking! She was through doing favors for men. She was not going to pass around her "goodies" anymore. Look where it had gotten her. She was nothing but cheap labor. She couldn't even get a marriage certificate to show for all her hard work. Now this Jewish fellow wanted her to get him a drink of water. And no wonder—he didn't have a pot or a cup. So he was going to use hers. Being used. She knew what that was like. She recoiled, "Not so fast, Mister."

Then she launched into a history lesson about the Jews and Samaritans. "We don't get along, let alone do favors for one another. So move on down the road, buddy. Ask someone else to be your servant. I won't do one thing for you."

Talk about a hostile encounter. Unfortunately, this is what happens when you have been told repeatedly you don't belong. The claws come out. The defenses go up. The adrenaline kicks in. Years of doing favors only to be met by years of rejection turned this woman into an animal ready to attack.

"Don't get near me or I'll tear you apart. I'm going to reject you before you have the chance to reject me."

But to her surprise, rather than tell her to get lost like everyone else had, this man's response took her off guard.

"I know all about you. And I love you anyway."

She stopped. Put her pot down. Rubbed her ears. Had she heard him correctly?

"To know me is to love me? I don't think so. Nobody ever told me that before. Whenever anyone gets to know me they want to get rid of me."

Then came the words she had longed to hear all her life: "You belong to me."

To everyone else she was a reject—she was a Samaritan, what's more she was a woman—a woman with a dubious track record. A woman with no husband, no family, no country, and no home. But this stranger at the well saw something else. He had just found one of his lost kids and wanted to bring her home.

This woman never knew anyone really cared about her. She never knew she had a family. She never knew she belonged to someone—permanently—that is, until the man at the well pulled out her birth certificate and told her to take a look.

It was a brave move on the part of a Jewish man asking a Samaritan woman for a favor. It was a compassionate move if you are a loving parent who just found your child and can't wait to take her back home to dinner with the rest of her family.

Our Need—His Response

Do you feel as though you don't belong? All alone in a great big world? Unwanted by family? Abandoned by a person who promised to love you until "death do us part"? Rejected by parents who are too busy with their own lives to make time for you?

Then you need to meet the man at the well. He is still searching for his lost children, the ones who have been cast off, the kids who think nobody cares.

In Matthew, the tender care of our heavenly Father is represented by a shepherd looking for a lost sheep. "If a man owns a hundred sheep, and one of them wanders away, will he not leave the ninety-nine on the hills and go to look for the one that wandered off? And if he finds it, I tell you the truth, he is happier about that one sheep than about the ninety-nine that did not wander off. In the same way your Father in heaven is not willing that any of these little ones should be lost" (Matt. 18:12–14 NIV).

Jesus longs to embrace you and bring you into his family circle, a place where you belong. And like the woman at the well, once we know we belong, we'll want to tell everyone. We'll want the entire town to meet our family. John puts it this way when he describes what the Samaritan woman told anyone who would listen: "Come meet the man who loves me just as I am. Come meet the family I didn't know I had," she shouted as she ran through town (see John 4:28).

Not even the disciples' condescending question to Jesus, "Why are you talking to her?" could dampen this moment. No one could rain on this parade. Gone was the woman's self-doubt. Gone was the concern

> It softened my heart with relief to find "You" had not rejected me. It pulled me toward encouragement to see "Your" confidence in my not failing.
>
> Martha Borth, mother, wife, friend, nurse, poet

about what others might say about her. Gone was the fear that nobody wanted her.

> There is no house like the house of belonging.
>
> David Whyte

She belonged to someone, and that made all the difference in the world. And it will make a difference in your life, too. For when we know we are family, when we know we belong, it changes everything.

I know because I saw what happened in my dad's life when, after years of searching, he was reunited with his own brothers and sisters. I remember the day our family pulled up in front of a red brick house in Elizabethton, Tennessee, and my dad came face-to-face with a brother he had never met—separated for over thirty years. What a moment of happiness as these two grown men hugged each other, tears pouring down their faces. My Uncle Crawford took my dad everywhere with him. He wanted everybody in town to meet his "baby brother." As these two spent time together, it was amazing how alike they were. They looked like each other. Laughed like each other. Even walked like each other.

Years apart could not erase the fact they belonged to each other, held by a family bond that time and distance could not break.

You belong too—to the man who loves all his children. He embraces everyone, no matter what their track record. He doesn't have favorites. He doesn't single out one child over another. He loves us all the same. In the beautiful words of St. Augustine, "He loves each one of us, as if there were only one of us."

You are held by a bond that will never be broken. You are part of a family. And Jesus will never reject one of his children.

Even if you feel broken down and used up like the woman at the well, because he is a loving parent, he will look for you every day. And when he catches the first glimpse of you, he won't regale you with reminders of your soiled past or

61

berate you lest your besmirched reputation tarnishes his good name. No, he'll run to you and throw his arms around you, shouting all the way, "She's home! She's come home! My child who was lost is found" (see Luke 15:20).

> See what an incredible quality of love the Father bestowed on us, that we . . . are counted the children of God.
>
> 1 John 3:1 AMP

A Time for Reflection

The Rejected Woman: Samaritan Woman at the Well
Background Text: John 4:5–42

Exploration

My thoughts on rejection . . .

1. Is there an experience in my life that left me feeling rejected?

2. Did a person reject me? Who was that person, and how did the experience make me feel?

3. How would I feel if I knew someone really cared about me?

4. To whom do I feel I belong?

   > All whom my Father entrusts to Me will come to Me; and the one who comes to Me I will most certainly not cast out. I will never, no never, reject one of them who comes to Me.
   >
   > John 6:37 AMP

Inspiration

> For I have not come to call the righteous, but sinners.
>
> Matthew 9:13 NIV

> I'm after mercy, not religion, I'm here to invite outsiders, not coddle insiders.
>
> Matthew 9:13 Message

Several years ago, a friend recommended a wonderful book called *Streams of Mercy* by Dr. Mark Rutland, president of Global Servants Ministries. He writes about a survey in which thousands of Americans were asked what they would most like to hear someone say to them. Here are the top three responses:

Number 1: "I love you."
Number 2: "I forgive you."
Number 3: "Supper's ready."

I love the observation Mark Rutland makes about these three unique responses:

> It dawned on me. That's the whole gospel. (*Good News*) Jesus stands behind the communion table with his nail-scarred hands outstretched and the light of mercy in His eyes. His voice, His words meet us with healing warmth as we drag our water-logged burdens up the rocky shoreline from life's most chilling seas. "I love you," He whispers. "I forgive you. Come and dine."[2]

Isn't this what the Samaritan woman at the well received from Jesus? She found someone who loved her; someone who had forgiven her; someone who invited her to drink at his well that never runs dry. "The water I give will be an artesian spring within, gushing fountains of endless life" (John 4:13 Message).

Who would have guessed that a five-time divorcee, now living with a man, would end up turning her town upside down for Jesus—but that is exactly what happened when a rejected woman found out she belonged—when she finally met her Father. "Now numerous Samaritans from that town believed in and trusted in Him because of what the woman declared and testified" (John 4:39 AMP).

1. If I had been the woman at the well, how would I have responded to Jesus's request for a favor?

2. What lessons can I learn from the woman at the well?

3. How can I accept Jesus's invitation to be part of his family?

4. How do I feel knowing Jesus invites me to eat at his table with the rest of his family?

> Our funky little church is filled with people who are working for peace and freedom, who are out there on the streets and inside praying, and they are home writing letters, and they are at the shelters with giant platters of food. When I was at the end of my rope, the people at St. Andrew tied a knot in it for me and helped me hold on. The church became my home in the old meaning of home—that it's where, when you show up, they have to let you in. They let me in. They even said, "You come back now."
>
> Anne Lamott, *Traveling Mercies*

Affirmations

> How blessed is God! . . . Long before he laid down earth's foundations, he had us in mind, had settled on us as the focus

of his love . . . Long, long ago he decided to adopt us into his family through Jesus Christ. (What pleasure he took in planning this!)

Ephesians 1:6 Message

This is and has been the Father's work from the beginning—to bring us into the home of His heart.

George MacDonald

Look at me. I stand at the door. I knock. If you hear me call and open the door, I'll come right in and sit down to supper with you.

Revelation 3:20 Message

Unfulfilled *(ún fú fíl'd)* adj.

1. Unsatisfied.

2. Marked by failure to realize or attain to full potentialities of experience or development.

5

The Unfulfilled Woman

And the twelve were with him, and also some women who had been healed . . . Mary, called Magdalene, from whom seven demons had gone out, and Joanna, the wife of Chuza, Herod's steward, and Susanna, and many others, who provided for them out of their means.

Luke 8:1–3 RSV

In high school I was fortunate enough to be recommended for an after-school job, a typing position in the laboratory at the local hospital.

Every afternoon when school was out, I walked a few blocks to work. The route I intentionally took went by the physicians' parking lot where I would take a moment to stop and drool over one doctor's powder blue Mercedes SL—my teenage dream car.

I fantasized about the day I would have enough money to get a car just like it. I pictured myself driving around town with the top off, my hair flying in the breeze.

Fifteen years later my dream came true. I was in San Francisco and had just sold a large account for the advertising agency I worked for. Driving away from the client meeting, I spotted "my" car in the window of an automobile showroom. It was a 1984 metallic blue convertible Mercedes 380 SL. The vehicle was used, but that did not matter to me.

It was the car of my youthful fantasy, and I wanted it. To my delight, my husband stopped at the dealership. He agreed the price was right, and within hours the car became mine. I was on cloud nine.

For the next two months, I would not let anyone touch the car. I might as well have moved into it. Top off—top on, I drove it everywhere. I was on a car honeymoon.

But all too soon the honeymoon came to an abrupt halt. Although the car's odometer registered only twenty-four thousand miles, it broke down a lot. During the first four months I owned the vehicle, it was in the repair shop three times.

Then the hammer fell. The transmission went out. When my husband came home from the auto shop, I could tell he was not bringing me good news.

"There's a small problem with your car," he began. (Somehow I didn't feel he was being totally up front when he used the word *small*.)

"The mechanic found a discrepancy in the mileage records," Jim continued. The bottom line: the car that looked so beautiful on the outside was a fraud on the inside. It did not have twenty-four thousand miles on it. The

The world is too much with us; late and soon getting and spending, we lay waste our powers; little we see in nature that is ours; we have given our hearts away; a sordid boon!

William Wordsworth, "The World Is Too Much With Us" (1807)

68

mechanic estimated it had been driven over one hundred thousand miles. He believed the odometer had been rolled back. My car was a used lemon.

In complete frustration I was finally forced to get rid of the car. Most of the time it wasn't running. And when I needed it, I could not depend on it. Frankly, by the time I traded the car for another more dull, yet dependable vehicle, I was glad to see it go. I had sold a big account, received a large commission, and gotten what I thought I wanted—the car that would make me happy. What a joke! My dream became a nightmare. The "thing" I wanted so badly did not bring me the fulfillment I expected.

Unfulfilled. Incomplete. Lacking.

Everyone has a dream, a crazy notion that takes our minds off the here and now and elevates us to the realm of the "what if." For me it was the vision of driving around in a powder blue convertible Mercedes. That dream kept me studying when my friends were out playing. I realized my family wasn't rich. Mom and Dad did not have the money to buy me any car, let alone a Mercedes. If I were to get what I wanted, hard work would be the price I would have to pay.

So what is your dream? And, if I may be so bold, what price are you willing to pay to get what you want?

Did you marry "Mr. Right" because he had a great job and a promising future and you thought your dream of a beautiful home would come true the day you said "I do"? Then life stepped in. The unexpected happened and like my friend Jackie, your husband died suddenly. Killed in a car accident. The mortgage on your beautiful home was too much for you to pay. You had to sell your fancy house and move into something cheaper. The insurance money was less than expected, so you had to go back to work. The salary at one job wasn't enough to make ends meet, so you were forced to take a

> Wise men and women in every major culture throughout history have found that the secret to happiness is not in getting more but in wanting less.
>
> Elaine St. James,
> *Simplify Your Life*

second. Your dreams have gone up in smoke. You are living in a small apartment, raising three kids, and you are all alone. This was not the life you dreamed about. And you ask yourself, "What went wrong?"

Not long ago, I listened as three women in their midforties talked with a prominent news reporter about their dreams. All three had graduated from well-known universities. After college they got the corporate jobs they wanted. Life was good. No, life was great.

All these ladies became successful beyond their wildest imaginings. Up the ladder they hustled. Marriage, family, kids—those desires could be put on the back burner. They had plenty of time in the future.

But now the future was today, and these three women had to face the stark reality: they had exchanged career success for childless, even loveless, lives. I felt terribly sad at how betrayed they felt over their predicament. Because of the choices they made, the time clock had run out on their dreams. They had paid a steep price to get what they thought they wanted. Unfortunately, now that the future was today, they decided the price was too high.

I don't know what dream you have, nor do I know what you are willing to pay to see your dream come true. But have you found the price is too much? Has your family suffered as you worked unbelievably long hours in order to get that big promotion? Has your health failed as you pushed yourself to the breaking point for a bigger paycheck? Are you living with a dream that started out as a "what if" but ended with an "if only"?

Sadly our society makes it easy for us to believe that our dreams of fulfillment will come when we acquire a certain car or live in a bigger home or have a larger stock portfolio. All of a sudden we find ourselves brainwashed into thinking that with just a little more of what we want, we will find the satisfaction we dream about.

In his thought-provoking book *The Virtues of Prosperity*, author Dinesh D'Souza debunks the myth that more means happiness. "Many people discover that material possessions, however abundant and engaging, do not satisfy their deepest longings. Without a sense of larger perspective, the pursuit of possessions can assume a tedious and even futile aspect, becoming in the end a joyless quest for joy . . . today more and more successful people are fully cognizant of the limits of materialism. They are searching everywhere for a sense of meaning, of purpose, of something higher to which they can devote themselves."[1]

Not long after we were married, my husband, Jim, was able to see his grandmother for the first time in many years. The family had been separated over twenty years earlier when Jim's parents left Cuba to give their children a better life in the United States. Choosing to remain behind with other family members, Jim's grandparents were unable to leave the country when Fidel Castro took over power.

Finally, after years of working through legal channels, Abuelita ("little Grandmother"), as she was called, was able to move to the United States. I will never forget the first time she visited Jim and me. We lived in a nice home that was perfect for a young couple starting out. Our house had three small bedrooms and two bathrooms—a total of 1,400 square feet. After Grandma walked around the house, she came back to the living room with a look of awe on her face. In her Spanish she said, "You must get lost in here. It is so big. And for only two people."

> The only ones among you who will be really happy are those who will have sought and found how to serve.
>
> Albert Schweitzer

What I had thought was a modest starter home was a mansion in her eyes. What to us was a stepping-stone on the way to something better was her dream come true. Her perspective was an eye-opener.

If your dreams have turned to ashes and you have not attained the fulfillment you envisioned, if you are disillusioned by the fleeting enjoyment of some material possession, then I think you will find Joanna's story enlightening. For if fulfillment is the result of having your dreams come true, and your dreams consist of possessing all the right things, I suggest we all copy Joanna's game plan down to the smallest detail, because from the outside looking in this lady had everything: family, fame, and fortune. You would think she would be the most satisfied person on earth. But then, you would be wrong.

The Lady with Clout

Joanna was, as they say, born into money. Growing up she had all she wanted. Her parents sent her to the right schools. She was invited to the right parties. And yes, she married the right guy.

When you run with the "elite" crowd you will most likely end up marrying Mr. Elite, and that is what happened to Joanna when she married Chuza.

He was a wealthy man with a great job. As steward or domestic administrator of the court of Herod Antipas, Chuza had his finger on the political pulse of Judea. What's more, the immense wealth he managed gave him power and he quickly became a man with a great deal of clout (see Luke 8:3 KJV).[2]

Talk about having it all! The perfect couple with the perfect life. A real Judean "Power Couple." What more could a girl want? Talk about having your dreams come true! Cinderella was in the coach with Prince Charming at her side and glass slippers on her feet.

But just when Joanna thought she had everything she wanted in the palm of her hand, the unthinkable happened. You know what I am talking about. The phone rings, or you get a letter in the mail, or, as in Joanna's case, you wake up one morning and don't feel so well. You pass it off as just the flu, nothing to worry about. But days turn into weeks and weeks into months. What was once a minor annoyance becomes a major catastrophe.

It wasn't long before Joanna realized she could not do the things she had done before. She didn't enjoy her fancy clothes. She couldn't go to the extravagant parties. And after a while the terrifying thought passed through her mind: Would there ever be a day when she would feel well again? She began to doubt it.

Fortunately, Joanna had enough money to get the best medical care possible. No stone was left unturned as she searched for a cure. Yet all her efforts proved futile. Joanna was finally forced to face the unthinkable: she might die. Her money, her prestige, her position could not help her now.

Then a friend told her a story that seemed unbelievable. A woman named Mary Magdalene had been healed. She had been possessed, some said, by seven devils, but now she was back in her "right mind." This news seemed impossible. But Joanna's friends said it was true. Mary had been out of her mind, and now she was clearheaded. And as the rumor mill around town went, Jesus, the teacher and healer from Nazareth, had performed a miracle seven times for Mary.

After months of trying every remedy, Joanna was at the end of her rope. She was ready to try anything. So, as a last resort, this woman with everything decided to try Jesus.

The Man Who Gives You Exactly What You Need

I can't tell you the time or the day or the place. I don't know how it happened. Did someone take Joanna to see Jesus?

Did he come to her home? Did she follow him to some secret location? We are not told.

But one thing I can tell you: an encounter occurred that rocked Joanna's world. An event took place that was so life-changing it turned everything in her past, present, and future upside down. Gone were yesterday's parties, yesterday's friends, and yesterday's hollow life.

Before Joanna was healed, all her possessions were pawns in her hand to get what she thought she wanted. But when she became sick, she found out the one thing she wanted most was not within her grasp. Good health could not be bought. The material things she was holding onto so tightly were worthless. They could not save her life.

All Joanna wanted was her health restored so she could have her old life back. But when she met Jesus, he had a better plan for her. He wanted to give her back her health so she could enjoy a new life, a life that put the needs of others before the wants of self, a life with meaning beyond anything she had imagined. And from the day Joanna was healed she used her money to fulfill the real purpose of her life. The Bible record leaves us with this picture of Joanna's new life: "out of her means she gave to take care of others" (see Luke 8:3).

Rather than give Joanna what she asked for, Jesus gave her what he knew she needed: a life where generous compassion trumps material expansion.

Our Need—His Response

In your search for fulfillment, have you found that the pot of gold at the end of the rainbow is filled with fool's gold? Has the promised allure of material possessions left you feeling cheated?

Why not give your dreams to the Man who knows exactly what you need, the Man who understands what would really make your life fulfilled?

He knows your heart. He recognizes your strengths. And he will give your life a purpose beyond anything you might have envisioned for yourself.

Never forget—God's destiny for you is not limited by earthly tunnel vision but is open wide to his unlimited heavenly vision. "Long before we first heard of Christ . . . he had his eye on us, had designs on us for glorious living, part of the overall purpose he is working out in everything and everyone" (Eph. 1:11 Message).

He doesn't see the pattern of a splintered past or present. He sees the promise of a marvelous future—boundless potential given by the Man with unbounded love for you.

"For I know the thoughts and plans that I have for you, says the Lord, thoughts and plans for peace . . . to give you hope" (Jer. 29:11 AMP). And in *The Message*, this same text reads, "I know what I'm doing, I have it all planned out—plans to take care of you, not abandon you, plans to give you the future you hope for."

Even if we wait until Jesus is our last resort as Joanna did, he will never turn us away. He will never disappoint us. He may not give us the "thing" we want, but he will always give us the fulfillment we long for. Just see what happened to Joanna. Not only did she get her health back, not only did she get to walk with Jesus, but Luke tells us that Joanna was one of the first individuals to hear from angels that Jesus was risen (Luke 24:10). She could give a first-person account of the greatest event in history. That's what following Jesus gave Joanna—a front-row seat at an empty tomb. I'm going to tell you something—that is real fulfillment!

If you and I could ask Joanna if she would have traded her place at the tomb for some Roman social event where drunken rulers with their legions of soldiers were celebrating the crucifixion

> The fragrance always remains in the hand that gives the rose.
>
> Heda Bejar,
> *Peacemaking: Day by Day*

of a "Jewish Messiah," she would look at us and say, "Are you crazy?" For once you have eaten at the sumptuous buffet table set by Jesus, who in their right mind would ever want to go back to eat at the world's dirty pig trough?

Won't you accept the invitation to "open your mouth and taste, open your eyes and see—how good God is"? (Ps. 34:8 Message). And then this beautiful text ends with this promise: "Blessed are you who run to him." Joanna found true fulfillment when she ran to Jesus. You and I will find the same thing too! "You have made known to me the path of life; you will fill me with joy in your presence, with eternal pleasures at your right hand" (Ps. 16:11 NIV).

> And we know that in all things God works for the good of those who love him, who have been called according to his purpose.
>
> Romans 8:28 NIV

A Time for Reflection

The Unfulfilled Woman: Joanna
Background Texts: Luke 8:3; 24:10

Exploration

My thoughts on finding fulfillment . . .

1. What is my dream?

2. How have I attempted to fulfill this dream?

3. What do I think would bring me the fulfillment I want?

4. What things am I hanging on to, hoping I can use them to get what I want?

76

Many persons have a wrong idea of what constitutes true happiness. It is not attained through self-gratification but through fidelity to a worthy purpose.

Helen Keller

Inspiration

He wasn't yet thirteen years old, but on this day, life would change forever for young Bill Wilson.

"Come take a walk," his mother told him. Once they came to the large concrete culvert that crossed a canal close to their home, she turned to her son and said, "I just can't do this anymore. You stay here." And she turned and walked away.

Three days later, a Christian gentleman who lived in the neighborhood saw Bill still sitting on a cold piece of concrete. He stopped and picked up the abandoned youngster.

To make a long, sad story short and happy, he took Bill to a Christian youth camp where the young boy, who had never stepped his foot inside a church, found Jesus. As Pastor Bill Wilson talks about this experience today, with tears in his eyes and a crack in his voice, he says, "I know it sounds crazy. It may be hard to explain. But at that camp, after hearing about Jesus, I felt for the first time in my life that Someone really loved me."

From this experience, Bill Wilson made the commitment to do for other kids what had been done for him. And so with an old car and a small trailer into which he piled all his earthly possessions, he took off to follow the call of Jesus. And this call took him to Brooklyn, New York, to a rat-infested neighborhood plagued by drugs, gangs, guns, and poverty. But when Jesus said, "Follow Me," Bill Wilson didn't argue. He didn't ask for a beautiful church building or a lovely parish home. He said, "I'll go where you want me"—even when it meant Bushwick Avenue!

That was twenty-five years ago. Today, you can still find Bill Wilson driving a bus every Saturday, along with other "bus captains" as they pick up kids in the "no-go" neighborhoods of New York City. Not only does Metro Ministries, through its programs, reach over twenty thousand kids a week, there are now similar projects in many countries around the world.

If you were to ask Bill Wilson to define the word *fulfilled*, I think it would take one sentence: "A *full* bus, *filled* with kids, on their way to meet Jesus."

The same offer of fulfillment is given today that was given two thousand years ago: "Come with me. I'll make a new kind of fisherman out of you. I'll show you how to catch men and women instead of perch and bass." And then Matthew continues with these words, "They didn't ask questions, but simply dropped their nets and followed" (Matt. 4:18–20 Message).

> The only true happiness comes from squandering ourselves for a purpose.
>
> William Cowper

1. If I had been Joanna, what need in my life would I ask Jesus to fill?

2. Are there "things" in my life that are holding me back from fulfilling God's destiny for me?

3. What do I think is God's purpose for my life?

4. Have I accepted his purpose for my life?
   If not, why not?

> The very first condition of lasting happiness is that a life should be full of purpose, aiming at something outside self.
>
> Hugh Black

Affirmation

A devout life does bring wealth, but it's the rich simplicity of being yourself before God.

1 Timothy 6:6 Message

Insecure *(in sî - kyõõr)* adj.

1. Lacking self-confidence.

2. Uncertain.

3. Lacking likelihood of permanence or success.

6

The Insecure Woman

> Then, on coming into Peter's house Jesus saw that Peter's mother-in-law had been put to bed with a high fever. He touched her hand and the fever left her. And then she got up and began to see to their needs.
>
> Matthew 8:14–15 Phillips

I laugh when I hear people refer to a couple who has been married only a few years as "soul mates." Frankly, I think the term is overused. To use this word to describe people who have experienced a brief love affair, untested by time or trials, is ridiculous.

If you want to meet real soul mates, then I'll introduce you to my parents. They met at the age of eight and ten; married at nineteen and twenty-one; and for the next thirty-eight years, until my father died, had lives intertwined as closely as any couple I have ever known.

My father's path crossed my mother's when, as a young boy forced to sleep outside on a cold porch in the winter,

The Lord is my Rock and
my Fortress and
my Deliverer.

2 Samuel 22:2 AMP

he routinely developed severe cases of pneumonia and was brought to the local hospital when his condition worsened.

There he became the patient of one of the few doctors in town—Dr. Pohle. And it was the doctor's good wife, my future grandmother, who took this orphan boy under her wing. She provided him with shelter and love in his world of turmoil and pain. She tutored him when school was difficult, mothered him when he felt unwanted, and guided him when his feet began to travel down the wrong path.

Little did she ever imagine that this boy would grow up to one day marry her daughter, but that's exactly what happened. Although as youngsters my future mom and dad couldn't stand each other, absence, in this case, did make their hearts grow fonder. While away at college in different locations, Jimmy and Ellen had a change of heart. After looking over the field, they decided the best person for a lifelong partner was right in their own backyard.

My sister and I are glad they settled on each other. We feel blessed to have parents who not only loved us but loved each other with an "everlasting" love. Defying the predictions everyone made, believing a doctor's daughter should not marry a poor orphan boy, my parent's successful union left naysayers shaking their heads.

They defined the term "soul mates," individuals whose childhood history and adulthood love held them together with a bond never to be broken.

My mother's strength provided the foundation my father needed after an unstable childhood. My father's outgoing personality was a beacon of light for my mother's shy nature—a melding of "two becoming one."

This is why my father's sudden death left a huge hole in Mother's world. The life they had known was blown apart in one fatal moment—no warning, no planning ahead.

At the time when two people were at their peak, looking ahead to many "golden years" together, my parents were torn apart by the cold hand of death, a hand that doesn't care if it deals its blow in the prime of life.

After the funeral, when guests had left and everyday life began to stare my mother in the face, she was forced to make decisions regarding her future. She did not want to live six hundred miles away from her daughters, so she sold the home she and my father had purchased only two months before his death. Since she didn't have a place to move, it was decided she would stay with my husband and me for a few months.

What was going to be a short stay turned into nearly two years, a time when the strong, independent mother I had known became uncharacteristically dependent on others. One day as we discussed her situation, Mother confided that she felt lost. Her role in life had changed. My father's life and hers were so closely aligned, his absence had left her without a compass. His interests were her interests, his work her work. And the same could be said about my father. His life, too, revolved around my mom. As Mother tried to explain, she felt an insecurity she had never known. She was unsure of herself. She was in uncharted territory, and it was frightening.

Insecure. Uncertain. Apprehensive.

I have talked to many people who express the same emotions my mother did. An unexpected crisis occurs in their lives, and they feel as though the rug has been pulled out from under them.

Events like a traumatic divorce, a catastrophic illness, the sudden death of a loved one, an unplanned move to a new location, or the untimely loss of a job can cause all of us to experience feelings of insecurity. These emotions leave us feeling unsteady, shattered by the present and fearful of the future.

Most of my life I believed feelings of insecurity were a sign of weakness. "Be strong," I would say to myself. "Face your trou-

> He is my Rock of unyielding strength and impenetrable hardness and my refuge is in God!
>
> Psalm 62:7 AMP

bles with courage. Pull yourself up by your own bootstraps." These were clichés I had heard, and I thought they worked. Little did I know. And so when my mother—our family's tower of strength—admitted to feeling insecure, I had to reassess my own point of view. Was insecurity the sign of weakness I thought it to be? Or was it a natural result of events beyond our control?

As I reviewed my personal response to the unexpected in my own life, I found to my surprise that what I saw as a lack of courage shown after unsettling events often proved to be a time of necessary readjustment, a time when stable footing was sought in unstable situations.

This point was driven home to me early on the morning of February 9, 1971. Our family lived in Los Angeles, just fifteen miles from the epicenter of the Sylmar earthquake.

I happened to be the only person up in the house that morning, and I was getting ready to go to school.

All of a sudden the earth moved—violently. Without warning cans of food and dishes flew around the kitchen, tossed from cupboards with such force the debris traveled across two rooms. My parents' grand piano skidded across the living room. Pictures flew off the walls. Furniture toppled over. What made the situation more frightful was that the shaking seemed to last forever.

Anyone who has experienced an earthquake will tell you that when the earth starts to shake, you are left with a great sense of insecurity. What's more, once the initial shock is over, you never know when another jolt will strike. It seems that just when your nerves calm down, an aftershock hits, leaving you on a heightened state of alert all over again.

After the earthquake, our family didn't want to leave the house. Whenever anyone ran an errand, we wanted to know where they were going "just in case." Every time the house moved, even when a door closed, we jumped, thinking we were in for more shaking, rattling, and rolling.

The insecure feelings that blanket us when we don't know what will happen next can cause us to build walls around ourselves, barriers to shield us from the unknown. We want to be protected. We don't want to feel off balance as life throws us curve balls, so we come up with all kinds of solutions. We install security systems in our homes. We build "lock-down" rooms, hoping they will keep us safe from thieves, bullets, storms, and even life. Some folks even hire security guards as just another attempt to help maintain a sense of safety.

Several years ago Faith Popcorn, a futurist who predicts societal trends for major corporations, coined the word *cocooning*. In her book *Clicking*, she makes this observation. "To protect ourselves from going crazy from distress-overload, we are building more psychological and emotional cocoons around ourselves every day."[1] She notes that "cocooning" is our attempt to shield ourselves from the trauma we experience on a daily basis.

Evidently the idea of cocooning is not new because I found a lady in Capernaum, over two thousand years ago, who tried to protect herself when her world was turned upside down. An unexpected crisis struck that left her feeling alone and insecure so she sought to bring equilibrium back into her shaky world.

I Feel the Earth Move

She was a dependent mother-in-law, relying on her family for food and shelter, counting on help from those who cared about her well-being. Her world was torn apart because of her husband's death, so she moved in with her daughter and son-in-law, Peter. No sooner had she begun to feel as though life was getting back to normal than everything fell apart—again. She became ill, extremely sick with a high fever of unknown origin. At this time in history, any illness could prove disastrous. The doctors could not figure out what to do. And this left her in a state of confusion with one unanswered question: "What does the future hold for me?"

Does this situation hit close to home? Are you forced to rely on others when you have always been able to take care of yourself? Or are you a caregiver who has accepted the responsibility of looking after someone who always provided for your security in the past? You feel as though you are caught in quicksand being sucked under fast. The present is unstable, and the future is frightening.

If you are feeling insecure about a crisis in your life, then you can relate to this mother-in-law. Without warning, her world moved. A dead husband, an unplanned move, an unexpected illness, more bills, more trauma, more questions, and more insecurity.

What was she to do? Well, she did what you and I do when we find the earth moving under our feet—we look for stable ground.

And this is exactly what Peter's mother-in-law did; she searched for *something* solid. But in this case, she reached out for help from *someone* solid. She asked her family to get word to Jesus and ask him to come immediately to her aid (see Mark 1:30–31 KJV).

She recalled how her son-in-law, Peter, had told stories about Jesus's calming stormy seas, bringing peace to the mentally tormented, and healing sick lepers. She hoped Jesus could bring some stability to her own storm-tossed life.

Without hesitation a message was sent. The feverish woman's family asked Jesus to come to their home. They went directly to the man they felt could take control of the situation. And Jesus did not let them down. I appreciate that he did not chide them for not showing enough strength to bear up on their own during this crisis. Rather, he dropped what he was doing and responded without delay.

The Man Who Is Our Solid Rock

Jesus had a busy day. He had delivered a lengthy sermon. His steps had been dogged by a multitude of people clamoring for his attention. All he wanted was some rest, so he turned to his friend Peter and said, "Let's take your boat across Lake Galilee. I want to go where things aren't so noisy. Perhaps I can take a nap at your house."

Relaxation was on Jesus's mind. But no sooner had his boat touched the shore near Capernaum than a Roman centurion asked him to heal his servant. That wasn't all. Peter's own family was in need of Jesus's prompt attention. Mom was ill, and Jesus must come quickly or she might die.

Just another day in Jesus's life. But unlike other times when Jesus waited to heal someone or appeared to take his time meeting their need, Jesus's response was instantaneous. No hesitation. No waiting for the right moment. When Peter's family saw their world rocked by the unexpected, Jesus moved quickly to lend a steady hand of help. He was the anchoring force they needed. Without delay his presence secured their world. Peter's mother-in-law was healed. In fact, within moments she was well enough to get out of bed and "minister" to them. As one author puts it, "She got up and cooked dinner." With Jesus's stable hand at the helm of her life, she could begin to do what she did best—pass on Jesus's love to others.

Our Need—His Response

Like this dependent mother-in-law, do you face unsettling events in your life? Does the future look foreboding? Has a tidal wave of insecurity swept over you, knocking you off your feet?

Then do what Peter's mother-in-law did: go to the Rock. When buffeted by the storms of life, when illness and death

> You are my Father,
> my God, and the Rock
> of my salvation!
>
> Psalm 89:26 AMP

left her feeling upended, Jesus's stable presence was her grounding force. As David so eloquently wrote in Psalm 18:2, "The Lord is my rock, my fortress, my deliverer, my strength, my trust, my high tower." That sounds like Someone who has a strong shoulder to rely on, whose steady hand will keep the world from spinning out of control.

When this sick widow needed security, Jesus was the "someone" she could trust. But that was not the only way Jesus steadied her world. He also gave her something to do. As soon as she was well, she began to find people whose needs she could meet. Jesus knew that one of the best ways we can conquer our feelings of insecurity is to meet the needs of others who are suffering. By assisting another person in need, we are able to shift the focus from our own problems to the needs of others.

As my own mother went to the "Rock" to find the anchoring she needed, she redirected her talents to teaching music, getting involved in community activities, and ministering to those who could benefit from her newfound strength.

If feelings of insecurity overwhelm you and the ground beneath you begins to move, go to the man who will stabilize your feet. Go directly to the Rock. Jesus will not let you down. Instead, he will come to your aid, giving you solid ground to stand on, a strong shoulder to lean on, and unwavering security you can rely on. "God is our refuge and strength, an ever-present help in trouble. Therefore we will not fear, though the earth give way and the mountains . . . quake. . . . The LORD Almighty is with us . . . God . . . is our fortress" (Ps. 46:1–3, 11 NIV).

> My life is . . . a mystery which I do not attempt to really understand, as though I were led by the hand in a night where I see nothing, but can fully depend on the love and protection of him who guides me.
>
> Thomas Merton

A Time for Reflection

The Insecure Woman: Peter's mother-in-law
Background Texts: Matthew 8:14–15; Mark 1:30–31; Luke
4:38–39

Exploration

My thoughts on feeling insecure . . .

1. How do I define the word *insecure*?

2. What event in my life left me feeling insecure?

3. How did I seek to cope with the feelings I was experiencing?

4. How do I try to alleviate my own insecurities?

5. When I feel insecure, to whom do I turn for help?

6. Why and what is the result?

> God keeps your days stable and secure—salvation, wisdom and knowledge in surplus.
>
> Isaiah 33:6 Message

Inspiration

When I was growing up, an exciting event in our family was going camping. I'll let you in on a little tip here. Camping is great fun if the trip is being taken with people who are experienced campers. Back when I was a kid, we couldn't afford a fancy RV, so camping trips consisted of our family's tent, tarp, and four sleeping bags. But we always had fun because my dad was a pro when it came to pitching a tent, hanging a tarp, or any other camp project.

For several summers, our family visited a campground in Oak Creek Canyon in Arizona, a place I still consider one of the most beautiful in the world. Back in those days, to get to the canyon we would take a long winding road that came through the Red Rock country of Sedona.

Little did I know that one day I would be fortunate enough to call Sedona home. But today, my husband and I can look out on those same majestic ore-filled mountains, and every evening as the sun sets, we watch those same rock formations go from red to pink and even purple as the sun says goodnight to the impressive canyon walls.

After living in Sedona a few months, a friend asked if I had ever been to the top of one of the large rock formations. I thought she'd lost her mind. "No one could hike up there." She laughed and said, "I meant have you ever taken a jeep ride up there?" I quickly pointed out that I don't like heights. But that didn't stop her cajoling, and finally one day, I found myself hanging onto the safety bars inside a jeep as we climbed our way to "the top of the world." At least that is how I felt when our jeep arrived at a level area on the top of the mountain which was not visible from the ground.

As I stood on a huge rock (an understatement), I felt a sense of awe and was reminded of King David, an outdoorsman, who was so overwhelmed by the mountains he viewed and the rocks he stood on that the only thing he could compare them to was the strength of God. Maybe this is why so many of the Psalms refer to God as the Rock of our strength. David found that when the earth moved under his feet, the Rock of Strength was the one he needed to call on.

I like to think of it this way. When I need security under my feet, I won't SOS the Coast Guard; I'll SOS the ROS (Rock of Strength). It's what Peter's mother-in-law did. It's what David did. It's what I'll do!

I run to you, God; I run for dear life. Don't let me down! Get down on my level and listen, and please—no procrastination! Your granite cave a hiding place, your high cliff aerie a place of safety . . . I've put my life in your hands. You won't drop me, you'll never let me down.

Psalm 31:1–5 Message

1. What lessons can I learn from Peter's family?

2. What events in my life do I need to call the Rock of Strength about?

3. How do I feel knowing I can call on God for strength?

4. Do I know someone who is feeling insecure? How can I help them?

> The Lord's our rock, in him we hide, a shelter in the time of storm . . . mighty rock in a weary land, a shelter in the time of storm.
>
> A Shelter in the Time of Storm, words by
Vernon J. Charlesworth, public domain

Affirmations

> From the ends of the earth I call to you, I call as my heart grows faint; lead me to the rock that is higher than I. For you have been my refuge.
>
> Psalm 61:1–3 NIV

> I will sing of your strength, in the morning
> I will sing of your love; for you are my
> fortress, my refuge in times of trouble.
>
> Psalm 59:16 NIV

Isolated (*ı' sa - lãt'd*) adj.

1. *Set apart from a group or whole.*

2. *Solitary.*

3. *Placed alone or apart.*

4. *Cut off.*

7

The Isolated Woman

And a great crowd followed him and thronged about him. And there was a woman who had had a flow of blood for twelve years, and who had suffered much under many physicians, and had spent all that she had, and was no better but rather grew worse. She had heard the reports about Jesus, and came up behind him in the crowd and touched his garment.

Mark 5:24–28 RSV

It had been a long and tiring trip. My husband and I were headed from Los Angeles to Phoenix, but we managed to squeeze in one more stop.

I had heard about Childhelp USA® and their nationwide Child Abuse Hotline, 1-800-4-A-CHILD. I knew Childhelp USA® was one of our country's oldest and largest organizations dealing with child abuse and neglect, and was aware they had a residential child abuse facility, but I had not seen the center myself. Since our drive home took us close to the loca-

Too often we underestimate the power of a touch, a smile, a kind word, a listening ear, an honest compliment, or the smallest act of caring, all of which have the potential to turn a life around.

Leo F. Buscaglia

tion, Jim and I called ahead and were invited to take a tour.

Having worked with non-profit organizations for over twenty-five years, I had visited many facilities that focused on the needs of children in crisis, so I was not surprised by the work Childhelp USA® does; however, I was amazed at how they do it.

The drive to the Children's Village took us across rolling green hills to a group of buildings surrounded by perfectly manicured grounds. Frankly, I could have mistaken the location for an exotic health spa.

Once inside, our tour guide took us through the classrooms, library, kitchen, and chapel. Then we went out to the barn where a variety of farm animals greeted us.

Lastly we were escorted to the individual "cottages." This is where my mouth dropped open. No institutional bedcovers. No cold bare walls. No worn-out couches. Instead, each living area was designed like a home. A living room with fireplace, comfortable chairs, a game table, and a dining room where everyone gathered for meals. But best of all there were beautiful bedrooms outfitted to delight the heart of any little girl or boy, decorated around a theme—some with Disney animals, others with Barbie dolls. And every child's bed was covered with his or her own selection of stuffed animals.

"I've never seen anything like this," I remarked to our guide, Lauren.

"Well," she replied, "it's a reflection of the ladies."

In this case "the ladies" refer to Sara O'Meara and Yvonne Fedderson, two women whose outer beauty is a reflection of their inner love.

These two ladies could have lived the "easy life." As young Hollywood starlets, they could have focused on their careers.

Instead they chose to champion children—the ones other people forgot. And it is their love and commitment that continues to be at the heart of everything Childhelp USA® does.

As one social worker told me, "When we have had tough financial times, the ladies never let the children go without anything. Everyone else tightens their belts, but the children always have what they need. The children always come first."

When I entered one of the cottages for young girls, a beautiful, blonde-haired child came toward me. She was a little girl who made me want to wrap my arms around her and take her home.

"What a gorgeous child. How could anyone ever abuse her?" I asked when my guide and I were alone.

I could see my question struck a particularly painful note, and the smile on the guide's face disappeared.

"I'll introduce you to her, but don't be offended if she doesn't respond."

"Why?"

"She's not yet seven years old," Lauren replied, "but already she has been in thirty-six different places."

I thought I hadn't heard her correctly. "What do you mean, thirty-six places?"

Lauren explained that this young girl was born to a mother who was addicted to drugs. She had been abused as a baby and put in foster care. Then her life really went downhill. As a "ward of the state" this baby was transferred from place to place. She spent an average of only two and a half months in each foster home or institution. After three months at Childhelp USA®, she had been there longer than any other place she had lived in her young life.

"We hope with lots of love and counseling to bring her out of her shell," Lauren continued, "but right now she doesn't want to be touched by anyone."

Isolated. Separated. Confined.

I still can't get the face of that young girl out of my mind, a precious child who had been so traumatized by hands of hurt she did not want to be touched by hands of love.

You may be able to relate to her. I don't know what kinds of hands have touched you, but if they were hands that delivered painful beatings or if they were hands that took away your innocence, you may feel like the young girl I met. Afraid. Alone. Fearful that anyone who gets near you might hurt you.

Recently, in Phoenix, a young boy was found locked away in a closet. His mother had chained him there like a dog. Medical specialists discussing the case admitted it would take years before this child could hope to recover from the emotional and physical damage he had sustained. Some experts acknowledged the young boy might never overcome the trauma he suffered at the hands of the woman who had given him life. The only touch he knew was one that brought terror.

Author Andrea Dworkei recognized the effect touching another person has when she penned these words: "Touching is the meaning of being human." We want to connect with another person, so we reach out and touch. A bond starts to form. We develop confidence. We begin to trust. And eventually we feel secure with this person.

But when that link of trust is broken and we are violated, we feel betrayed. We recoil in horror. Sometimes we even retreat into a world of silence, pain, and isolation.

If ever you were hit in anger by a parent, slapped by a spouse, molested by a relative, or sexually assaulted by a date, this destructive touch may have driven you into a world where you are afraid to connect—for connection brings pain and rejection.

This may be the life you are living. If so, there is someone you need to meet, a woman who had not felt the warmth of a human touch for twelve long years. She had been separated from her family and friends because she was unclean. She was segregated from society, fearful that if she had contact with any person she would defile them. Talk about feeling isolated—she was an expert on the topic.

> Jesus reconstructs expertly
> and it's His healing touch
> I squirm delightedly over.
> When His actions assure me
> that we're still friends.[1]
>
> Martha Borth, wife, mother,
> friend, nurse, and poet,
> *Sitting at His Feet*

Don't Touch Me—I'm Dirty

This woman's trouble began when she started bleeding. At first she didn't give the problem a second thought. Women of child-bearing years bleed every month. And so, in compliance with the Levitical laws that defined behavior during the time a woman was considered "unclean" or "polluted" or "impure," she refrained from contact with anything or anyone.

But when the bleeding didn't stop she began to get worried. She visited the doctor. He wasn't certain what the problem was. She paid his bill. The bleeding still didn't stop. So she went to another doctor, and he couldn't diagnosis the problem. She paid him too. This vicious cycle went on for twelve years. That's right. Twelve years of a daily flow of blood. Nothing stopped the problem. No one had an answer.

I can't paint this picture any more grimly than it was. This woman's life was a big list of no's, beginning with no touching. That meant no cooking, no cleaning, no entertaining, no socializing. Then there was the temple—she could not go there. She would pollute the space. And worst of all, her condition ruined any hope for a normal family life. She couldn't touch her children or her husband. No hugging. No kissing. No affection. No sex. The bottom line . . . no touch . . . no life!

And what about all the repeated trips to solicit a cure? Mark laid out the result of her efforts: "she suffered much under many physicians, and spent all that she had" (Mark 5:26 RSV).

Not only had she evidently undergone every medical procedure known, she'd spent all her money on a futile endeavor, to the point where she was flat broke. Once the money ran out, so did the medical attention. Her health was no better and her heart was still broken.

As the years crept by, hope disappeared, along with relationships. It was impossible to feel close to people she couldn't touch.

Then one day someone told her Jesus was coming to town. And they added this piece of information that was pertinent to her case: Jesus "touched" people. The very ones society called unclean. He laid his hands on people with fevers. People who couldn't see or hear.

The best news of all—he even touched lepers. The most ostracized beings on earth were welcomed by his outstretched hands. Hope began to boil in her heart. "Maybe this man will touch me too," she prayed.

The Man with the Healing Touch

Jesus was passing through town at the request of a man named Jairus, a ruler of the synagogue. His twelve-year-old daughter was sick, and he was hoping Jesus would heal her. I am certain, if I had been Jairus, I would have wanted Jesus and the crowd that was following him to keep up the pace. "Hurry, hurry," I might have said. "Don't waste a minute. Every second counts. Can't you speed things along?"

Then all of a sudden Jesus came to a dead stop, not what Jairus wanted at all. "Who touched me?" Jesus inquired. Even the disciples thought the question absurd. Mark described the scene this way: "a great crowd kept following and pressed Him from all sides so as almost to suffocate Him" (Mark 5:24 AMP).

But this touch was different. And Jesus, "recognizing in
Himself that power proceeding
from Himself had gone forth,"
turned to find the person who
in faith was trying to reconnect
with another person. Not just
any person, but the one person

> Christ touches you, and His
> touch is so delightful that,
> more than ever, you are
> drawn inwardly to Him.
>
> Madame Jeanne Guyon

she believed could touch her and heal her in the place that
hurt the most.

This woman might have to crawl on her belly like a snake.
She might have to overcome the fear of being trampled to
death by the crowd. Worse yet she might get caught for breaking the rules and touching another person. But the promise of
healing was worth the risk of trying. And in a desperate move,
her outstretched hand touched the fringe of Jesus's coat.

She knew it was a risky move. She knew she should not
touch anyone. And once her act was exposed by Jesus to the
onlooking crowd, she recoiled in fear. She was certain she
would be punished. Isn't that what happens to you if you do
something that upsets the apple cart? Hands of hurt teach
you a lesson you won't forget.

She waited. Would she feel the sting of a hand of hurt?
Would she be thrown out of town? Instead the hand that
reached down to her had only one intent, and that was to
lift her up. At the moment when this woman felt exposed to
the world, at the most vulnerable time in her life, the healing
hands of Jesus brought cleansing to her body and soul.

There's one more little detail in this story that is easy
to overlook. Not only did Jesus's touch heal the woman's
disease, but then with one word Jesus restored her to the
family. "Daughter," he said to her, "your faith has made you
whole." Other family members may have abandoned her—
Jesus had not.

There has been only one male person in my life who has
called me "daughter," and that was my dad. I remember

when I was six years old and he took me to a father-daughter banquet at the local Kiwanis Club. I was introduced to the city mayor, the bank president, and several other community leaders as "Jim's daughter." I thought I was so cool. I belonged to this man who knew all these important people. "Daughter" was my father's term of endearment.

And now, after losing touch with family and friends, this woman understood that she was still Jesus's daughter. Even after years of isolation, she had not lost touch with her Father.

The woman who had been confined—was now released. The woman who was isolated—was included. The woman who was separated—was connected at last.

When Jesus touched this woman she found healing, not hurt. In Jesus's presence she found the safety she sought and the healing she longed for.

Our Need—His Response

Do you feel isolated because of some painful experience in your life? Have you retreated into a world of hurtful memories? Are you afraid to reach out and form a bond with anyone because of a betrayal by someone you thought would never hurt you?

Jesus invites you to reach out as the sick woman did. When she came to Jesus, he recognized she needed more than a cure for her physical pain. She needed restoration from her emotional pain. She needed healing for the heartbreak caused by years of separation and isolation. This is why Jesus offered her the warmth of a human touch and the affection of a Father who loved his daughter.

Jesus invited the woman into the safety zone of his love. To paraphrase the words of the

In the deserts of the heart let the healing fountain start.

W. H. Auden

poet Edwin Markham, "He drew a circle that took her in." And that circle is large enough to include every woman who has ever felt isolated and afraid, separated and alone. It includes every woman who has endured the harm caused by hands that deliver torment, rather than tenderness.

Jesus understood this woman's needs because, as the apostle Paul so eloquently wrote, "He has been touched, himself, by the pain that touches us" (see Heb. 4:15). He felt the hate of someone spitting in his face. He winced as a whip cut into the flesh on his back. His head ached as a crown of thorns was shoved into his skull. He knows what pain is all about. When you hurt, he hurts too. When you feel isolated and alone, he is there to bring comfort and healing.

This is why he welcomes you into his circle of love, a place where you can receive healing—his healing touch. This is the reason so many people came to Jesus, asking him to touch them. Mothers longed for him to touch their children. The sick asked him to touch their bodies. The distressed cried out for him to touch their hearts. The isolated wanted his touch to help them form a bond of trust. For those in pain, Jesus's love was a healing love, a safe haven in a world of hurt. And when we enter a place of safety, we become free to find healing for the broken places in our lives. "Unto you who revere . . . my Name shall the Sun of Righteousness arise with healing in His wings . . . and you shall go forth . . . released" (Mal. 4:2 AMP).

For you alone make me dwell in safety and confident trust.

Psalm 4:8 AMP

A Time for Reflection

The Isolated Woman: The Woman with a Hemorrhage Background Texts: Matthew 9:20–22; Mark 5:25–34; Luke 8:42–48

Exploration

My thoughts on feeling isolated . . .

1. What do I think of when I hear the word *touch*?

2. In what types of instances am I afraid to connect for fear of rejection?
   Why?

3. What event in my life caused me to feel isolated?

4. How did this event make me feel?

5. Has there been a time in my life I could not connect with others because of the pain I suffered at the hands of another person?

6. What have I tried to do to reconnect and overcome my fear?

> They sent word to all the surrounding country. People brought all their sick to him and begged him to let the sick just touch the edge of his cloak, and all who touched him were healed.
>
> Matthew 14:35–36 NIV

Inspiration

Jesus reached out his hand and touched the man.

Matthew 8:3

Jesus touched her hand and the fever left her.

Matthew 8:15

Jesus touched their eyes . . . and their sight was restored.

Matthew 9:29–30

Jesus came and touched them . . . He said, "Don't be afraid."

Matthew 17:7

Filled with compassion, Jesus reached out his hand and touched the man . . . immediately the leprosy left him.

Mark 1:41–42

Who Touched Me?

We all bleed, we bleed for ourselves—
we each have our private pain, we bleed
for others; and we bleed for a wounded world.

If we did not bleed for others in some measure,
would we not be spiritually barren?
Unfit for our calling, incapable of conceiving
and nurturing new life, forming relationships
and caring communities.

But if the pain takes over and the bleeding
becomes constant do we not then find that
we have lost touch with our Lord?

He is obscured by the crowd of our concerns,
the crowd of our activities, the crowd
of our own words.

Jesus, help us to touch you now,
to lay before you our own and the
world's pain. Help us as we wait in
silence to feel your healing hands upon us.[2]

Consultation of Methodist Women
Ministers, Oxford, 1984

1. In what places in my life do I long to feel the healing touch of Jesus?

103

2. How would I have reacted had I been in the shoes of the lady who touched Jesus?

3. Is there a "safety zone" where I feel protected?

4. Where is it and why do I feel safe?

> Now you've got my feet on the life path;
> all radiant from the shining of your face.
> Ever since you took my hand,
> I'm on the right way.
>
> Psalm 16:11 Message

Affirmations

> Hold me up, that I may be safe.
>
> Psalm 119:117 AMP

The name of the Lord is a strong tower, the righteous run to it and they are safe.

> Proverbs 18:10 NIV

Lord of Healing

> Lord of my darkest place;
> Let in your light.
>
> Lord of my greatest fear;
> Let in your peace.
>
> Lord of my most bitter shame;
> Let in your word of grace.
>
> Lord of my oldest grudge;
> Let in your forgiveness.
>
> Lord of my deepest anger;
> Let it out.

Lord of my loneliest moment;
Let in your presence.

Lord of my truest self—my all;
Let in your wholeness.

Alison Pepper

Hunger *(hŭng'gar)* n.

1. *The discomfort, weakness, or pain caused by a lack of food.*
2. *A strong craving or desire.*

8

The Hungry Girl

He took her by the hand and said to her, "Talitha, koum," which means, "Little girl, I tell you to get up!" She got up at once and started walking around. (She was twelve years old.) When this happened, they were completely amazed. But Jesus gave them strict orders not to tell anyone, and he said, "Give her something to eat."

Mark 5:41–43 GNT

As I pulled into the parking lot at World Opportunities International, there was an old pickup blocking the driveway. I saw Dave Phillips, director of Gifts-In-Kind for the organization, standing by the loading dock, so I asked, "Do you know who owns that truck, Dave?"

"Yes," he answered, and then inquired, "Have you ever met Mae Raines?"

When I replied that I had not, Dave made quick work of seeing that I was introduced to the legendary "Bread Lady."

It didn't take long before I found out why everyone loved Mae. What a smile! And she had sparkling eyes you could never forget.

As Dave and I walked over to where Mae was standing, I could see her truck was being filled with packages of English muffins and bags of fresh fruit and produce.

"What's Mae's story?" I asked.

This is what I was told.

After watching children in her South Central Los Angeles neighborhood run the streets and become involved with gangs, Mae made up her mind to do something. But how do you tackle such a huge problem? Mae decided she would start her campaign in the place she knew best—her own neighborhood.

She began by opening her home to kids where she lived—a safety zone in a war zone. Kids were soon stopping by every day. However, it did not take long before Mae recognized that while youngsters needed the guidance of a stable figure in their lives, many of them faced an even greater problem.

They were not getting enough food to eat. Most of the kids never had breakfast.

Lunch was what they got at school. And in the summer, when school was out, lunch became optional, too. Going to bed hungry was a common occurrence.

Mae settled on a plan to tackle the hunger problem first. She had an old truck with a large flat bed. It was not much to look at, but it ran. Mae counted on her truck to help her get the job done.

She began searching for an organization that could help her with her endeavor and found World Opportunities International, Inc., a relief organization that collected surplus food and medicine,

> The question of bread for myself is a material question. But the question of bread for my neighbor is a spiritual question.
>
> Nikolai Berdyaev, Russian philosopher

108

then distributed them to needy neighborhoods in Los Angeles and around the world. She called the headquarters office in Hollywood and received just the needed encouragement. "Yes!" They had food. "Yes!" She could have what she needed.

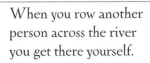

When you row another person across the river you get there yourself.

Anonymous

That was all it took for Mae to start her own neighborhood feeding program. She began by providing kids with one simple item: bread. Every week when she came to World Opportunities she arrived right after the day-old bags of Thomas's English muffins were delivered. As soon as the bread truck pulled away, Mae's truck pulled in. Packages of muffins were loaded into Mae's truck, and away she went back to her neighborhood and hungry youngsters.

One day Mae gave me an invitation I had been hoping for. "Dorothy, why don't you come to my house and meet my kids—all fifty of them?" I jumped at the chance.

A few weeks later my husband, Jim, and I took a map and made our way through the unfamiliar streets of South Central Los Angeles.

When lunchtime arrived, I stood on Mae's porch and watched kids pouring out of houses up and down the street—running to Mae's home.

On her front lawn, Mae had a picnic table loaded with bread, peanut butter, jam, and fresh fruit. It was a sight to watch over fifty kids fill her yard. Of course, Mae was right in the middle of the excitement, slapping peanut butter on bread, and hugging each child.

This is how Mae Raines came to be known as the "Bread Lady." When she found hungry kids—she gave them something to eat. When she saw a need—she used what she had to meet it.

But that isn't the end of the story. Turn the clock forward fifteen years. The young Dave Phillips, who saw to it that

Mae Raines got the food she needed, now heads up his own charity, Children's Hunger Fund. When corporate America came calling, desirous of Dave's organizational and people skills, he turned his back on a big salary and generous perks and took on the challenge of starting an organization from the ground up. Having seen the great need of food for hungry people, Dave decided to shoulder the immense responsibility of doing what he could to help solve the problem. Since Children's Hunger Fund opened its doors in 1992, the organization has distributed nearly one hundred million pounds of food worldwide and over a half billion dollars worth of medicine that has saved the lives of thousands of children and adults.

Just like Mae, Dave Phillips saw a need, and now he is using his talents to meet the desperate cry of millions of people.

Hungry. Malnourished. Starving.

Have you ever gone to bed hungry? I'm talking about a hunger that gnaws away at the pit of your stomach, a hunger that makes it impossible for you to think about anything else, a hunger that drives you to steal for a morsel of food, a hunger that destroys your life.

While I have never experienced this type of hunger, I know people who have. And they tell me, as unbelievable as it sounds, that after being deprived of food for extended periods of time, their longing to eat slowly went away as their bodies turned inward, nearly destroying themselves.

It is easy for us to believe that severe hunger doesn't hit people here in the United States. We may think malnutrition is limited to third-world countries, far from our shores, our towns, our neighborhoods, our homes.

But this isn't the case. Hunger hits people in America, too, now more than ever. What makes the problem so critical is that most of the time hunger in this country goes unnoticed. We think it can't happen here, so we don't look for it. Yet like a lurking tiger, hunger crouches in the shadows waiting to pounce on unsuspecting, helpless victims: little children, older folks, and families who find themselves in difficult economic situations.

> If you want to lift yourself up, lift up someone else.
>
> Booker T. Washington,
> civil rights activist

Several years ago, I was working as a volunteer in Los Angeles for a group that was delivering Christmas food boxes to hungry families. I remember taking a box to a single mother, who lived in a run-down apartment building. When I handed an orange to her small son, he looked at me with a puzzled expression and asked, "What is this?" I was shocked.

He had never seen an orange before. Maybe he thought I had given him a ball. I took the orange and showed him how to peel it. Then I broke off a section and handed it to him. I had to tell him it was OK to eat it. Soon orange juice was squirting out of the corners of his mouth and dripping down his chin. All he could say to me after experiencing his first bite was, "More!"

Right now one in five children here in our country live at or below the poverty level. This is an astonishing fifteen million children! If you ask people who work in food banks, they'll confirm that nearly 40 percent of all their food recipients are children. Sadly, the numbers aren't decreasing; they are skyrocketing.

What's worse, the effects of hunger on youngsters are devastating. Children who don't get enough to eat are known to have more health problems; learning is more difficult; and, not unexpectedly, the death rate is much higher.

In her soul-stirring book, *The Joy of Loving*, Mother Teresa put a face on hunger by sharing the touching story of one small child she met. "None of us, I am sure, knows what is the pain of hunger, but one day I learned it from a little child. I found the child in the street and I saw in her face that terrible hunger that I have seen in many eyes. Without questioning her I gave her a piece of bread, and then I saw that the little child was eating the bread crumb by crumb. I said to her, 'Eat the bread.' That little one looked at me and said, 'I am afraid because when the bread is finished I will be hungry again.'"[1]

More than once I've said to myself, if only there were a solution, a simple way to alleviate the scourge of hunger, or a miracle that would suddenly make enough food appear.

But while I was hoping the miraculous would happen, the answer was right under my nose, a blueprint for solving the hunger crisis, and it was left by a man with a vision for finding answers to tough problems. You'll find his solution in a story about one kind man's desire to give both a loving father and a sick little girl what they needed most.

So if like Mae Raines and Dave Phillips, you want to help alleviate the blight of hunger, keep reading. You are about to be called into action because your hands are urgently needed.

Daddy's Little Girl

From the day Tabitha was born, Jairus could not think of anything or anyone else. He was a father who had always dreamed of having a daughter. His joy knew no bounds when his dream came true. Devotion to his child filled his life. Every time he thought about Tabitha—his "little gazelle," as he called her—his eyes filled with tears. She was the love of his life.

You can understand that the day she became ill, Jairus's world came to a halt. Without hesitation he put all his energy into getting her well. He took her to the best doctors, but the doctors did not have an answer and his little girl didn't improve. For Jairus, a worried father, mild concern turned into paralyzing fear.

As the days turned into weeks and Jairus's child did not get well, this father's desperation turned to panic. Twelve-year-old girls aren't supposed to die. Yet every time he looked at his sick child, Jairus realized the worst could happen. He decided he must find someone who could save his little girl.

Fortunately, because of the elevated position Jairus held as a ruler of the synagogue, elected by community elders, he received information that others might not have. And in this case, it meant he knew where Jesus was. Immediately he dropped what he was doing and headed for Capernaum.

Just as he arrived and got Jesus's attention, though, a sick woman stopped the entire crowd. A delay in getting help. This must have been frustrating for this father. But things quickly deteriorated when news came that Jairus's daughter had died. A minor irritation caused by another person's need became a major tragedy with devastating consequences.

It was too late. His daughter would not get well. There would be no happy ending to this story. But Jesus's response to the news was completely the opposite of what the crowd expected. While the messengers were telling Jairus not to bother Jesus anymore, Jesus turned to the distraught father and delivered this message, "Do not be seized with alarm and struck with fear; only keep on believing" (Mark 5:36 AMP). And then, with his three closest disciples, Peter, James, and John, Jesus asked Jairus to lead the way to his home.

Strange. Jesus going to see a dead girl.

But grief-stricken Jairus was not in the mood to argue. He took Jesus directly to his home. As the group approached the house, they could hear family and friends wailing.

"Take me to her room," Jesus requested.

And then, as he looked at the lifeless body lying on the bed, Jesus spoke these words: "Little girl, I tell you to get up." That was all he had to say, and Tabitha obeyed.

The Man Who Asks for Your Help

A father's request answered, a need supplied. But there's more. Jairus wasn't the only person in this story who had a need. There was another person with a need, one that had not been met. And the person was a child. There was a young girl in the room who was hungry, a little one who needed something to eat.

Jesus could easily have solved Tabitha's hunger problem by giving her food. He'd done it before. He'd fed thousands. But he didn't choose to feed this child himself. On this day in the home of Jairus, Jesus met the need of a hungry child by turning to the people in the room and telling them, "Give her something to eat."

In the record of Jesus's life, there are seven different times when he provided food for the hungry. Twice he performed spectacular miracles—feeding thousands with a meager supply of fish and bread. He even took care of seeing to it that a wedding feast did not run out of wine.

So why didn't Jesus perform a miracle for Tabitha? He could have snapped his fingers and set a plate of food in front of this hungry child. There's no question he had the power to provide her with food, but instead he asked the people surrounding the girl to help her.

Just why do you think Jesus was so eager to enlist the help of others when it came time to feed a hungry child? I believe it was because he knows you and I will find the needs of our own hearts met when we reach out and help others, especially the most helpless—children, who can't care for themselves. "If thou draw out thy soul to the hungry, and satisfy the afflicted soul; then shall thy light rise in obscurity and thy darkness be as the noon day: And the LORD shall guide thee continually, and satisfy thy soul in drought, and make fat thy bones and thou shalt be like a watered garden, and like a spring of water, whose waters fail not" (Isa. 58:10–11 KJV).

The other people in the room did not have the power in their hands to raise young Tabitha from the dead. Jesus had that power, and he used his hands to do what he alone could do. Then he asked the others in the room to use their hands to do what they could, and that was to feed a hungry child.

Our Need—His Response

There are still hungry children in rooms around us, in streets around us, and in countries around us. The same man who asked for hands to help feed Tabitha calls out to you and me. He needs our help. He needs our hearts to care and our hands to feed. He asks us to have, as the Hebrew dictionary so expressively defines compassion, "gut-wrenching concern" for the hungry.

This kind of compassion gets me out of a chair, makes me roll up my sleeves, and motivates me to get busy using my hands to help.

One of my favorite stories is about a man who was granted a vision of the afterlife.

He was first shown a great hall with a long banquet table filled with ambrosial delights. Each diner was equipped with a three-foot-long spoon, but no matter how much they contorted their own arms, thrusting their elbows into their neighbors' faces, their utensils were too long to maneuver even a single morsel into their gaping mouths. They sat together, opposite and side-by-side, in mutual misery.

"This," said the man's otherworldly guide, "is Hell."

The visitor was then taken to another place and saw an identical banquet table set with the same sumptuous food and the same impossible silverware. Only here the residents were well fed, utterly joyous, glowing with health and well-being.

"This," pronounced the host, "is Heaven."

The man was baffled. "What's the difference?"

"In Heaven," said the guide, pointing delightedly as a person lifted his long-handled spoon across the table to the parted lips of a neighbor, "they feed each other."[2]

What could happen if thousands of people, like Mae and Dave, did what they could, with what they have, right where they are? What if we followed the example of the people in Tabitha's room and when Jesus said, "She's hungry, give her food to eat," we answered, "Here are my hands. I'll help."

I was hungry and you fed me. I was thirsty and you gave me a drink. I was homeless and you gave me a room. I was shivering and you gave me clothes. I was sick and you stopped to visit. I was in prison and you came to me . . . I'm telling the solemn truth; whenever you did one of these things to someone overlooked or ignored, that was me—you did it to me.

Matthew 25:35–40 Message

A Time for Reflection

The Hungry Girl: Jairus's daughter
Background Texts: Mark 5:21–43; Luke 8:41–56

Exploration

My thoughts on hunger . . .

1. How can I help alleviate the problem of hunger?

2. What organizations could I support to help feed the hungry in my community?

3. Why are my resources important to share?

4. How could I volunteer to help in my community?

5. Why is my time important to share?

> I have one life and one chance to make it count for something . . . I'm free to choose what that something is, and the something I've chosen is my faith. Now, my faith goes beyond theology and religion and requires considerable work and effort. My faith demands—this is not optional—my faith demands that I do whatever I can, wherever I can, whenever I can, for as long as I can with whatever I have to try to make a difference.[3]

> Jimmy Carter, president of the United States of America, Bible study teacher, Habitat for Humanity volunteer

116

Inspiration

What I'm interested in seeing you do is: Sharing your food with the hungry, inviting the homeless poor into your homes, putting clothes on the shivering ill-clad, being available to your own families.

Isaiah 58:7 Message

This past year, an eighty-year-old man named John van Hengel died.

His body was not flown to Washington DC so he could lie in state at the Capitol Rotunda. Throngs of people didn't walk by his casket. No world leaders gathered to pay tribute. He was laid to rest the same way he lived his life—as a quiet, common man. Yet in his lifetime, he did more to relieve hunger around the world than any other person I know.

I will never forget my first meeting with John. I was helping raise money for St. Mary's Food Bank, the first and oldest food bank in the United States. I had been warned that John was a blunt guy who didn't tolerate nonsense. So I had my questions written down ahead of time.

My first question was, "How did you get the idea for a food bank?" I should have kept my big mouth shut and stopped to let him do the talking. But I continued, "What was your vision for the organization?"

He gave me one of those over-the-top-of-his-glasses scowls and said, "Vision. Are you crazy? There was no vision thing. Don't give me that bull____!" Then, sensing my surprise, he relaxed, gave me a smile, and continued. He had gotten my attention. But what's more, he taught me an important lesson.

As we talked, John didn't tell me about some grand corporate master plan. He didn't show me a business model that had food banks serving thousands of local agencies in cities across the country.

Instead, he boiled one man's life work down to a few sentences: "I saw hungry people going without food. I saw grocery stores throwing out food that had dates near expiration or packages with tears or cans with dents. The food was edible; the stores could not sell it. All I did was help bring the hungry and the food together."

In John's mind he hadn't done a great work. He thought he had done what anyone would do when they saw a need.

In 1976, John van Hengel left St. Mary's Food Bank to establish Second Harvest, an organization that would serve a consulting purpose to others interested in starting food banks. Today, now called America's Second Harvest, the organization is comprised of a network of more than two hundred food banks and is the largest domestic hunger relief organization in the country. When John saw a need he filled it. He said, "Here are my hands, use them."

> There is a marvelous story of a man who once stood before God, his heart breaking from the pain and injustice in the world. "Dear God," he cried out, "look at all the suffering, the anguish and distress in your world. Why don't you send help?" God responded, "I did send help. I sent you."
>
> David J. Wolpe, *Teaching Your Children About God*

1. Who are the hungry children in my neighborhood, my child's school, my church, or my own circle of family and friends who need me to feed them?

2. What would my answer be to Jesus when he said, "Give them something to eat"?

> The spirit, I think, is a stream, a fountain, and must be continually poured out, for only if it is poured out will more and clearer streams come.
>
> Brenda Ueland (1939), *Me*

118

Affirmations

This is the kind of fast I'm after: to break the chains of injustice, get rid of exploitations, free the oppressed, cancel debts. What I'm interested in seeing you do is: sharing your food with the hungry, inviting the homeless poor into your homes, putting clothes on the shivering, ill-clad.

Isaiah 58:7 Message

God has no hands or feet or voice except ours, through these He works.

Teresa of Avila

The Birth of Jesus

Born among the poor on a stable floor,
cold and raw, you know our hunger,
weep our tears and share our anger
yet you tell us more, born among the poor.

Every child needs bread till the world is fed:
you give bread, your hands enable,
all to gather round one table.
Christmas must be shared,
every child needs bread.

Son of poverty shame us till we see
self-concerned how we deny you,
by our greed we crucify you
on a Christmas tree, son of poverty.[4]

Shirley Murray, New Zealand

If my hands are fully occupied in holding on to something, I can neither give nor receive.

Dorothee Sölle, *Women of Faith & Spirit* (1987)

Worried *(wŭr′ éd)* adj.

1. Mentally troubled.

2. Distressed.

3. Concerned.

The Worried Woman

Then some little children were brought to him,
so that he could put his hands on them and
pray for them. The disciples frowned on the
parents' action, but Jesus said: "You must
let the little children come to me,
and you must never stop them."

Matthew 19:13–15 Phillips

There is an old saying, "You can choose your friends but not your relatives." How true. None of us has a choice when it comes to the family we are born into, and the same can be said when we get married. The extended family comes with the person we love.

In my case, I fell in love with someone whose family was a bonus—a loving, close-knit group who embraced me as one of their own.

As the years have gone by, my heart has become intricately entwined with my sister-in-law, Irma, to the point where we have dropped the term "in-law." We are sisters in every sense of the word. We have borne each other's burdens, shared each other's joys, cried over each other's failures, and rejoiced at each other's triumphs.

Since I did not have children of my own, Irma generously shared her two children with me. We vacationed together, spent holidays, birthdays, and graduations together. Her kids even lived with us for a school year while their family was moving from one city to another.

As my niece Jennifer and nephew Scott grew up, my husband and I were able to revel in the pleasure of watching them mature. Jenny became a nurse, Scott a computer programmer. Our family grew again when Scott married Kathy. He could not have chosen a lovelier girl. On a summer day in July, under large walnut and eucalyptus trees, surrounded by family and friends, Scott and Kathy were married. After the festivities were over, they left for their honeymoon in Cancún, Mexico. It was the perfect beginning for a young couple's life, a life filled with plans and dreams, brimming over with enthusiasm and expectation.

Just three months later, however, on a Saturday morning, our phone rang. It was Irma, sobbing uncontrollably. I could not understand the words she was saying, but after asking her to repeat herself, the news became all too clear.

"Scott has been sick the past few days," she began. "We thought he had the flu, so he went to the urgent care. After drawing some blood and doing a chest x-ray, they sent him directly to the hospital. The doctor says he has a large tumor in his chest, and his blood tests are abnormal. They think he has acute leukemia."

> Making the decision to have a child—it's momentous. It is to decide forever to have your heart go walking around outside your body.
>
> Elizabeth Stone

Within hours the diagnosis was confirmed. Scott was transferred to a large hospital in Los

122

Angeles and immediately placed on a regimen of chemotherapy, treatment that would hopefully put him into remission and eventually a cure.

Without warning, his young life, so full of promise, was turned upside down. And Irma, the mother who was overjoyed by the recent happiness in her son's life, now worried constantly, hoping her child would live to enjoy each new day.

Over the next few months, while Scott's wife began her job as a second grade teacher, Irma took time off from work to transport Scott to chemotherapy sessions. The entire focus of Irma's life was on helping her child get well. Her first thought in the morning was how Scott was doing, and her last thought before she dropped off to sleep at night was a prayer for his recovery. Scott's welfare was her total concern. Worry was a constant companion, leaving Irma worn out during the day and enduring many sleepless nights.

Worried. Troubled. Concerned.

What are you worrying about right now? Has the recent loss of a job been keeping you up at night? Are you wondering how you are going to pay the bills? Has the illness of an elderly parent left you anxiously trying to figure out how to balance their care and your workload? Or like Irma, are you worrying about a child facing a serious illness?

Let's admit it, worry is part of our lives. Like a stalker, worry tracks us down, keeps our nerves on high alert, and fills our minds with troubling thoughts.

Unfortunately, worry doesn't evaporate into thin air when we click our heels together and hope for the best.

If, like the song says, we could "pack up our troubles in an old kit bag and smile," life would be easy. But I ask you, have your problems disappeared by hiding them in a suitcase? Neither have mine. Trouble has a way of finding us. Even more sinister, trouble has a way of reinventing itself as new problems hatch each day. How appropriate that author Paul Sullivan portrayed worry as "a snake that would lay eggs in my brain." A frightening visual image of an emotion that causes injury to both mind and spirit.

Charles Horace Mayo, one of the founders of the world-renowned Mayo Clinic, offered this perspective on the impact worry has on us. "Worry affects the circulation, the heart, the glands, the whole nervous system. I have never known a man who died from overwork, but many who died from doubt." You may be able to relate to his statement. Perhaps you need a new pair of shoes because yours are worn out from going to the medicine cabinet to get a pill to help you sleep at night or a drink of something "chalky" to ease the pain in the pit of your stomach.

Of course it does not help when every time we turn on the radio or watch television, we hear about wars, the threat of "dirty bombs" blowing up, or the scare of some health crisis like the bird flu. With so much to frighten us, it is no wonder advertisers take advantage of our fears and bombard us with ads for preparations that relieve ulcers, stop headaches, or end insomnia, ailments often caused as a result of worrying. If only a magical medicinal preparation would make our worries go away! Yet I have never heard of a pill that eliminates worry. If anything, trying to survive in such a complex world has only increased our anxiety level.

To prove my point, I recently keyed the word *worry* into my computer and punched "search" just to see what I would find. To my amazement, there were over 6,490,000 references that contained the word *worry*.

What surprised me most was how many of these sites dealt with worry in the context of family issues. Parents are con-

> We have to fight them daily, like fleas, those many small worries about the morrow, for they sap our energies.
>
> Etty Hillesum,
> *An Interrupted Life*

cerned about the safety and well-being of their children. Children are worrying about the health of their elderly parents. And families worry about financial stability.

Once the word *parent* enters your personal description, the reasons to worry dramatically increase. This may be why Jesus took time to address the topic of worry. And he did so by acknowledging the concerns of a group of mothers with children. It is an act that should not be passed over lightly by women who find themselves overwhelmed by anxious thoughts for a sick baby, or for a child who is struggling in school, or for a teen who is taking drugs.

There When We Need You

In one of my favorite old movies, *Teacher's Pet*, starring Clark Gable and Doris Day, a hard-nosed city newspaperman played by Gable advises his young protégé that when you want to get a complete story you should ask six questions: Who? What? Where? When? How? Why? And in order to understand a brief encounter that took place one day in the life of Jesus, we need to do the same.

The who, where, and how are answered in one sentence. A group of mothers, hearing that Jesus was teaching on a mountainside, brought their children to him so he could bless their little ones.

This act on the part of parents was not a new concept in Jewish culture. For hundreds of years, parents had brought their children to the temple to be blessed by the priests. Raising your child to be God-fearing was essential to good parenting. Asking for a blessing on your child was one way parents kept foremost in their minds the weight of the task they were given.

But now, let's ask the why, what, and when questions. Why did the mothers come to Jesus? What made them think he was a person who could help them raise their children? Why not go to the temple as other parents had done in the past? And finally, why did these mothers come to Jesus when they did? What made them bring their children to him at this specific moment?

It is important to remember that the mothers who asked for Jesus's help had a lot to worry about. Jewish families at this time in history lived in occupied territory. The province of Judea was ruled by a ruthless Roman governor and over-run with Roman soldiers. Add to this burden an unjust tax system that brought chaos to the financial well-being of the people. What's more, the rigorous religious system of the day was so weighed down with minute details and excessive laws that rather than bring relief to troubled hearts, it added more burdens.

No wonder these mothers were troubled. And it is no sur-prise they were searching for something or someone who could help them shoulder the load they carried.

So why Jesus? And why now? In order to find the answer to these questions we need to back up a few days and take a second look at a crucial incident that left an indelible mark on the memory of the people in Galilee. I maintain this event motivated the moms to seek Jesus. It certainly would have made me think Jesus could handle anything.

The circumstance I am referring to was a trip Jesus's friends took across the Sea of Galilee late one evening. Without warn-ing a severe storm whipped up such violent waves it appeared all the boats on the lake would capsize.

All of a sudden in the middle of the lake, a lone figure appeared, walking on the water toward one of the boats. Suddenly, the disciples recognized the form was Jesus. With a calmness that belied the terrifying situation, Jesus spoke three words: "Peace, be still." Within seconds, tranquility returned to the lake. A wave of Jesus's hand and the sound of his voice brought the disturbance under control. To the disciples who were frightened that they would not live to see another day, Jesus became the master of their fears because he held sway over the circumstances that petrified them.

Imagine the stories being spread after this adventure on the lake. I can hear people recounting in exact detail Jesus's ability to bring the elements of nature under control. If I had been a concerned mother with children I loved, my thinking would have gone something like this: *If Jesus can bring peace to the forces of nature, I know he can take control of the turbulence in my life.* If you are an anxious mother apprehensive about the diagnosis of cancer for a son, fearful about the influence of the wrong friends on your teenage daughter, or nervous about how you will pay the bills this month, you can arm yourself with the knowledge that if Jesus could battle the billows, he can handle your problems too.

> People get so in the habit of worry that if you save them drowning and put them on a bank to dry in the sun with hot chocolate and muffins they wonder whether they are catching a cold.
>
> John Jay Chapman

The Man Who Gives Us Peace

Jesus's public life was filled with a crush of people. Like a rock star, he had fans. Five thousand people at a time would follow him, showing up on a mountainside or waiting for his arrival by the Sea of Galilee.

His was not a restful life. And on the day the moms and kids arrived, Jesus had other company. The religious leaders showed up to ask him questions. It was time for Jesus's handlers to step into the fray. So his friends, the disciples, decided they would engage in crowd control. They would serve as Jesus's time managers. In the hierarchy of the crowd, moms and kids did not rank high on the list of "Things for Jesus to Do."

When the disciples saw the mothers and little ones, they emphatically told them to "get lost." According to the disciples' plan for the day, Jesus must use his time and energy to impress the theologians, not the housewives. Thankfully, Jesus was paying close attention and spoke up, putting an abrupt halt to the arbitrary decision making employed by the disciples.

Instead of telling the moms and kids to step to the rear, Jesus ushered them to the head of the line. They were first in his kingdom and his heart. Jesus knew the job of parenting is one of the toughest jobs there is. He understood parents need the strength of Superman, the tact of Mr. Rogers, and the wisdom of Solomon. Hands that rock the cradle have heads that worry.

This is why Jesus stopped what he was doing and offered both his hands to mothers: one hand to bring peace, the other to lift burdens.

Our Need—His Response

Did you lie awake last night tossing and turning because of a problem that appears insurmountable? If a crisis has turned your world into a storm-tossed sea, take your concerns to Jesus. The man who brought quiet to a storm can bring peace to your life. He gave us his promise: "Peace I leave with you, my peace I give unto you . . . Let not your heart be troubled, neither let it be afraid" (John 14:27 KJV). As one author wrote, "Peace is not the absence of conflict, but the presence of God no matter what the conflict."

The warmth radiating from hands that invited careworn mothers to his side are also the

> Worry is like a rocking chair—it keeps you moving but doesn't get you anywhere.
>
> Corrie ten Boom, *Prison Letters*

tender hands that were laid in blessing on the children. And those same hands have the strength to lift our burdens and the power to calm the uproar caused by the tempest swirling in our lives.

There is a song, recorded by the Brooklyn Tabernacle Choir, which features the voice of Alvin Slaughter. Written by Steve Adams, it is titled "Peace in the Midst of the Storm." When I have found my life battered by uncontrollable storms, the moving rendition of this song has a way of lifting me above the turmoil. I find great solace in these beautiful words:

> When the world I've been living in crumbles at my feet,
> When my life is all tattered and torn;
> See I've been windswept, I've been battered,
> but I'll cling to the cross,
> He gives me peace in the midst of a storm.
>
> He gives me peace in the midst of a storm,
> He's my anchor, He's my rock I can build my faith
> upon;
> Jesus Christ, He's my refuge, in Him I can hide,
> He gives me peace in the midst of the storm.[1]

I know it is easy when the waves are crashing around us to forget that the hands that calmed a raging storm can bring serenity to our world no matter what we face. As a daily reminder I keep this note taped to my desk:

Today I will be handling all your problems. Please remember, I do not need your help. If a situation you cannot handle happens to appear, DO NOT attempt to resolve it. Kindly put it in the SFJTD (Something For Jesus To Do) box. It will be addressed in MY time, not yours. Once the matter is placed into the box, DO NOT hold on to it or attempt to remove it. Holding on or removal will delay the resolution of your problem. If it is a situation that you think you are capable of handling, please consult me in prayer to be sure that it is the proper resolution. Because I do not sleep nor do I slumber, there is no need for you to lose any sleep. Rest my child. If you need to contact me, I am only a prayer away.

Author Unknown

Why not put your worries in the SFJTD box today? Jesus invites you to "Pile your troubles on God's shoulders—he'll carry your load, he'll help you out" (Ps. 55:22 Message). This is a promise that gives me peace of mind, and a good night's sleep!

My perfect love will cast away all your fears.

Jesus

Worry never robs tomorrow of its sorrow, but only saps today of its strength.

A. J. Cronin

A Time for Reflection

The Worried Women: Mothers with Children
Background Texts: Matthew 19:13–15; Mark 10:13–16; Luke 18:16–17

Exploration

My thoughts on worry . . .

1. What do I worry about most?

2. Has my worrying solved the problem?

3. What do I do to relieve the worry in my life?

4. Are there events in my past, present, and future that I worry about?

> Peace I leave with you;
> My peace I now give and bequeath to you . . .
> do not let your hearts be troubled,
> neither let them be afraid.
>
> John 14:27 AMP

Inspiration

> Hush now! Be still! And the wind sank as if exhausted . . . and there was immediately a perfect peacefulness.
>
> Mark 4:39 AMP

One of our favorite family pastimes in the Arizona summer was taking my grandpa's boat to the lake for a day of waterskiing.

In the evening, after wearing ourselves out all day skiing, my dad would take my sister and me and any friends we had brought along on a slow, quiet ride around the lake.

On one particular trip to Apache Lake, when our evening ride began, we chose to go up the lake to the point where there was a large dam. It was twilight as we got to the farthest point from our camp, and as we turned around to begin our leisurely trip back, the boat engine began to sputter, then stall, and finally it just died. Quiet. Not a noise. My dad tried to restart the motor, but all attempts were futile. There we were, with the impending darkness, stuck on a lake. My sister and I glanced at each other with that look of panic that says, "Oh, no, what are we going to do?" At nearly the same moment, we turned to see our dad pulling something out from the front of the boat. A set of oars! We had no idea there were oars on the boat, but my dad did. Unknown to us, he had stocked the boat with a set of oars, an emergency first-aid kit, extra food and water, a small inflatable dingy, flares, and a huge flashlight. I can't tell you how relieved we were to know the man in our life, our dad, had planned ahead. He didn't consider our situation an emergency because he had packed what we needed in case everything didn't go as planned. The Man in your life and mine has planned ahead too. He knows what challenges you will face. He knows what worries will trouble your heart. And he has promised to have on board all the supply of strength you need. "My grace is enough; it's all you need. My strength comes into its own in your weakness" (2 Cor. 12:9 Message). It certainly makes a difference when the captain of your ship knows exactly what to do!

1. Like the mothers who brought their children to Jesus, have I brought my family to Jesus?

2. What help would I ask him for?

3. Have I asked Jesus to give me his peace?

> One who is anchored firmly in God does not suffer any loss, even if attacked by a thousand waves and a thousand storms. On the contrary, [she] emerges stronger.
>
> John Chrysostom, *On Providence*

Affirmations

> Then they cried out to the Lord in their trouble, and he brought them out of their distress. He stilled the storm to a whisper; and the waves of the seas were hushed. They were glad when it grew calm, and he guided them to their desired haven.
>
> Psalm 107:28–31 NIV

Jesus, Savior, pilot me over life's tempestuous sea; unknown waves before me roll, hiding rock and treacherous shoal; Chart and compass come from Thee; Jesus, Savior, pilot me.

"Jesus Savior, Pilot Me," words by Edward Hopper, 1871, public domain

Ignore *(ig-nŏr)* v.

1. To disregard deliberately.

2. Pay no attention to.

3. Refuse to consider.

10

The Ignored Woman

Leaving that place, Jesus withdrew to the region of Tyre and
Sidon. A Canaanite woman from that vicinity came to him,
crying out, "Lord, Son of David, have mercy on me! My
daughter is suffering terribly."

Matthew 15:21–22 NIV

The date was December 24. I had just arrived home after fin-
ishing my Christmas shopping. Unwrapped gifts were stacked
on the dining room table, and I was in a hurry to get to my
parents' house for our traditional Christmas Eve supper.

In my rush, I laid a stack of mail on the edge of the kitchen
counter, and as I did, an envelope marked Radiology Department fell to the floor. Earlier in the week I had gone for my
annual mammogram, but I was not expecting the results of
my test to arrive so soon.

> The reason why we have two ears and only one mouth is that we may listen the more and talk the less.
>
> Zeno of Citium, Greek philosopher

I tore open the envelope and my eyes fell on the words, "Please call us immediately." Panic struck. I continued reading. "You have an abnormality on your mammogram. We tried to reach you by phone but there was no answer."

After finding a phone number on the letter I held in my trembling hands, I got the office on the telephone. I gave the receptionist my name and was transferred to a technician, who informed me that I needed to set up an appointment with a surgeon. "We think you may have cancer," the person on the other end of the line stated in a matter-of-fact tone. I don't know about you, but the "cancer" word destroyed my day. I was frightened. I was scared. I began to cry. Not wanting to ruin Christmas for my entire family, I told my husband about the results, but I did not let anyone else know until after the holiday.

Once Christmas festivities were over, I needed support. I called my mom, my sister, my best friend, and several female co-workers. I was a wreck. The threat of having breast cancer consumed my days and nights.

A flood of thoughts filled my head. Will my breast have to be removed? Will I have to take chemotherapy? Am I going to die? If you have faced a similar situation, you know what I was experiencing.

Fortunately, my sister, Sheryl, who is a nurse, knew about a special center that treated breast disease. She was able to make an appointment for me to see the head physician, a renowned specialist. There was just one problem. The doctor did not have time in his schedule for three weeks. Needless to say, those weeks became the longest of my life.

I know everyone who knew me became tired of my obsessive behavior. I could not think about anything else. I didn't want to talk about anything else. Everyone tried to ease my mind by saying, "Why don't you wait and see what the tests reveal? Not all lumps are cancerous."

They might as well have been talking to a wall. Their kind words didn't help. All I knew was the doctor who read my X-ray thought I had cancer.

After days of regaling anyone who would listen to my tale of woe, I noticed people were not paying as close attention anymore. They would smile, nod sympathetically, and say, "Yes, Dorothy, we know. You have told us before." While I felt as though people were not paying any attention, the fact was, those around me were unable to solve my problem.

Finally, one of my friends said, "I hope you don't think I'm being rude, but I can't talk about this anymore. I'm not helping you at all."

She was right. She couldn't change things. Her honesty made me realize that as much as I was haranguing everybody with my concern, there was nothing anyone could do until I went to an expert for help. I needed to go to someone whose training provided them with the ability to make an accurate diagnosis and treat my problem.

Ignore. Disregard. Overlook.

For a while I thought I was the only person in the world who could become so wrought up over an event in my life. It wasn't long before I found out I was not alone.

In fact, you may be one of my soul sisters, someone who has faced a similar experience. As I discussed this situation with other women who had abnormal mammograms, I found they experienced the same fears I did. One woman told me, "My family didn't know what to do for me. I fussed and fumed for days. I was paralyzed with fear."

When a crisis strikes our lives we can become so focused on that single situation that nothing else matters. And it doesn't have to be an abnormal test with the diagnosis of cancer hanging over our heads. It can be the rebellion of a child, grief at the death of a parent, betrayal of an unfaithful spouse. All these circumstances and more can stop us in our tracks, leaving us emotionally incapacitated.

When the trauma of life pushes us to the breaking point, we long to find someone who cares, someone who will provide comfort, and, most of all, someone who will listen. All too often, those around us are busy with their own lives. Challenged by their own difficulties, they don't have time to solve our problems, let alone listen to us complain about the misery we are going through. So we feel ignored. We become paranoid. We may even think, *nobody cares about me and my problems.*

The other day I was in Toys-R-Us and a cute little boy, who looked about four years old, was trying with all his might to get his mother's attention. She had obviously met a friend and was attempting, unsuccessfully, to carry on an adult conversation. It was impossible because her young son was tugging on the hem of her skirt, hollering, "Mommy, Mommy, can you hear me?"

Of course, she could hear him. So could everyone else in the store. It didn't matter to this child. He wanted his mother to respond, now. At that moment in his life, she was the one person who could meet his need, and he wanted her entire focus to be on him.

There have been times when I felt like this little boy. I cried out at the top of my lungs, hoping I would be heard. I wanted my need to be met. I longed for someone to listen to me. Have you ever felt the same way? If so, you will be able to identify with a woman who felt completely ignored after years of crying out for help. She had a severe problem, a sick child. And no one seemed to care.

Everyone in town had heard her story. Now they just thought she was bothering them, rehearsing the details again and again. So they ignored her. She thought no one was listening. What she didn't know was that Someone was listening. In fact, this man's ear was tuned directly to her frequency. Her pleas showed up on his radar screen. And in response, he showed up on her doorstep.

A Little Puppy in a Big Dog's World

She was a Canaanite woman living on the northern frontier of Palestine. Mark called her a Syro-Phoenician after her country of origin. Her culture, religion, and language were most likely Greek.[1]

But on this particular day none of this mattered. She was a woman who needed to find a solution for a severe problem . . . a problem that was not of her own choosing. Her young child was afflicted by what some thought was epilepsy.[2]

Somehow—from somewhere—the news got to this foreigner's door that there was a healer in Israel, a Jewish prophet who was accomplishing the miraculous. There was only one problem: he didn't live in her community. He wasn't part of her world. Her chances of getting Jesus's attention were slim, especially since Jesus had never before crossed the border into Phoenicia. But when everything looked the darkest, the Son appeared on the horizon. Jesus came to town. He came to a foreign land, and into a foreigner's home.

Thankfully, you and I should never underestimate what Jesus will do to meet

> It is the province of knowledge to speak and it is the privilege of wisdom to listen.
>
> Oliver Wendell Holmes,
> *The Poet at the Breakfast Table*, 1872

> Listen, my children, with the ear of your heart.
>
> St. Benedict

our needs. And in this case, he had to walk for three days on a long, dusty road from point "A" to point "B," from Judea to Phoenicia.

A frantic mother's miracle was about to happen. The fact is she was one of a very few people in Jesus's life who understood what he meant when he said, "Your Father knows what you need before you ask him" (Matt. 6:8 NIV). She believed Jesus was her only answer, and all I can say is, she certainly got that right.

When news began to circulate in her village that Jesus had arrived, she realized her moment of opportunity was knocking. She had to get to Jesus, who had quietly slipped into a home for some much needed "R and R." However, rest was not on the agenda this particular day.

This desperate mother decided to become part of the Syro-Phoenician Welcoming Committee. But instead of greeting Jesus all prim and proper, with gifts in hand, she employed a different technique. She made her debut screaming. Hollering at the top of her lungs. Shouting above the noise of the crowd, "Have mercy on me, Son of David" (Matt. 15:22 KJV).

It did not embarrass her if people thought she was crazy. She needed help for her daughter. And you know how concerned mothers respond when their sick children require help. They'll turn the world upside down to get what is needed. I ask you, what length would you go to if your child were at death's door, or had been suffering year after year? I am certain you would have screamed too.

This mother, however, was in for a surprise. All her yelling did not get the result she intended. Jesus kept walking, acting as though he were oblivious to her. He appeared to be like all the other people in her life who ignored her. Matthew went so far as to describe Jesus's behavior this way: "He did not answer her a word" (Matt. 15:23 NIV). Silence. Not a sound. No response.

Since this mother was no shrinking violet, she persisted. She screamed even louder. Then she began to chase Jesus. She was not going to let him get away easily.

Picture the commotion. A large crowd is moving along the coastline, followed by a woman with a big mouth and a loud voice, yelling, "Help! Have mercy on me! Stop! Can't you hear me? My daughter needs you! I am not going to give up. I am going to keep calling out until you answer me. Jesus, I have nowhere else to go! Everyone else is ignoring me. I won't let you ignore me too."

The woman's undignified behavior may not have appeared to get Jesus's immediate attention, but it certainly got her noticed by his friends. The disciples had plenty of trouble keeping Jesus's reputation intact. The last thing they needed was for word to get around that a shrieking woman was stalking him. Even worse, a Gentile woman. They had to take decisive action.

"Jesus, tell her to stop. Send her away," they pleaded. "Order her to get lost!" (see Matt. 15:23).

Strangely, Jesus's response seemed heartless. He turned to the disciples and said, "I was sent only to the lost sheep of the house of Israel" (Matt. 15:24 NIV).

Wait one minute! Was Jesus sent only for "special" people? Was this the way he operated? Were there only a few select individuals who benefited from his concern? Or does he really hear every cry that is lifted to him, no matter how feeble?

The disciples breathed a sigh of relief. Hadn't Jesus selected them? They were the special ones, not this obnoxious foreigner. This lady was out of her league. Jesus would not take time for her or her people. But the disciples and everyone else had a big lesson to learn that day.

At this moment in the story, after the disciples urged Jesus to send the woman away, you might think this mother would feel so rebuffed she would have turned and left. Instead, in the very next verse we find her kneeling and worshiping Jesus, praying these simple words: "Lord, help me!" (Matt. 15:25 AMP). Jesus answered her, "Should I take bread from the big dogs and throw it to a puppy like you?" This wasn't a rude response. It was a response that exposed the unkind, exclusionary thinking displayed by the disciples who thought they were the elect, the chosen. This bold mother was ready with her own comeback, "Yes, some people think you are only here to meet the needs of the chosen, but even little puppies are allowed to lick up the crumbs that fall from the Master's table."

This dear mother only wanted help for her child. She did not ask to be invited to sit down for a scrumptious meal at Jesus's table in the dining room and act like a big shot. Just give her crumbs on the back porch. That's all she wanted. She did not need all of Jesus's attention; she would be satisfied with the leftovers. Anything Jesus did for the little puppy would be fine with her.

The Man Who Always Listens to You

And how did Jesus respond to the trust this mother put in him? The only way he could. "O woman," he said, "your faith is something else. What you want is what you get!" And the Bible says, "Right then her daughter was made well" (Matt. 15:28 Message).

If you read this story as recorded by Matthew and Mark, you will find this mother was the only person Jesus helped on this trip. I believe it is likely he traveled to foreign soil just to help her, because he knew she was ready and waiting for him. And he rewarded her faith.

Everyone in town had heard this mother plead for help, but she had cried so often her petitions became irrelevant. Her screams blended in with the common sounds of everyday life. Hers was another voice in a choir of needy people.

Jesus heard something different, because he listens like no other person in the world. Jesus recognized her voice because his entire focus is on people in need. All of his attention was aimed in this mother's direction because he is always ready to assist the helpless—wherever and whenever they call out to him.

> Holy listening—to "listen" another's soul into life, into a condition of disclosure and discovery may be the greatest service that any human being ever performs for another.
>
> Douglas Steere,
> Quaker writer

But something else happened in this story. Not only was a mother's child healed, but something changed inside the mother too.

Once she recognized Jesus was listening to her, she calmed down. She was no longer obsessed with the idea that her daughter had to be healed. Instead, she began to trust that anything Jesus did would be the best for her child. Jesus's listening ear directed this mother toward his ability, rather than her need. She was able to go from an attitude of "You have to heal my daughter" to "I'll trust whatever you do for my daughter." What a wonderful change took place in this woman when she understood how willing Jesus is to listen and help! She had an immediate attitude alteration. This is how author Oswald Chambers describes what happens when we take our needs to Jesus: "Every time we pray our horizon is altered, our attitude to things is altered, not sometimes but every time." A faithful mother reached out to a faithful healer. Her cry for help touched the man who listens, and her need was met in more ways than she ever dreamed. "The Lord is near to all who call upon Him, to all who call upon Him sincerely . . . He also will hear their cry and will save them" (Ps. 145:18–19 AMP).

Our Need—His Response

Have you been crying out? Hoping someone will hear you? If, like this desperate mother, you feel ignored, then do what she did—take your request to Jesus. Rather than seeking the assistance of bystanders who are busy trying to survive their own problems, ask for help from the man whose ear is always tuned to your voice. He is listening all the time. In fact, he invites us to call upon him, and he promises we will find him. "Call to Me and I will answer you and show you great and mighty things" (Jer. 33:3 AMP).

These reassuring words, so beautifully penned by one author, remind us that all our needs are met by a receptive heavenly ear:

> Keep your wants, your joys, your sorrows, your cares, and your fears before God . . . you cannot burden Him; you cannot weary Him . . . take to Him everything that perplexes the mind . . . nothing is too great for Him to bear, for he holds up worlds . . . nothing that in any way concerns our peace is too small for Him to notice. There is no chapter in our experience too dark for Him to read; there is no perplexity too difficult for Him to unravel. No calamity can befall the least of His children, no anxiety harass the soul . . . no sincere prayer escape the lips; of which our heavenly Father is unobservant, or in which he takes no immediate interest.[3]

How encouraging to read the words in James 5:11, "The Lord is very pitiful and of tender mercy" or as *The Message* paraphrases these words, "God cares, cares right down to the last detail."

And if you don't believe me, just ask a Gentile mother who was stuck in a foreign land without anyone who would listen to her, except one man who was three days and miles away. He was listening all the time. His attention was focused on her and she didn't even know it. And when no one else heard her, he did! "She called upon me, and I answered her; I was with her when she was in trouble; I delivered her; and I honored her request" (see Ps. 91:15). That same Man will do the same for you and me.

> Behold, the Lord's hand is not shortened at all, that it cannot save, nor His ear dull with deafness, that it cannot hear.
>
> Isaiah 59:1 AMP

> When someone deeply listens to you, your bare feet are on the earth and a beloved land that seemed distant is now at home within you.
>
> John Fox, *Finding What You Didn't Lose*

A Time for Reflection

The Ignored Woman: A Canaanite Mother
Background Texts: Matthew 15:21–28; Mark 7:24–30

Exploration

My thoughts on feeling ignored . . .

1. In what instances have I felt like no one was listening to me?

2. How did it make me feel?

3. Who do I go to when I need someone who will listen?

4. How does it make me feel to know someone is listening?

With listening comes the gift of healing.

Catherine Doherty

Inspiration

That's why I urge you to pray for absolutely everything, ranging from small to large. Include everything as you embrace this God-life, and you'll get God's everything.

Mark 11:24 Message

I heard it was red—a telephone that sat on the desk of the president of the United States and served as a direct line to the Kremlin during the cold war. I don't know if the phone existed. Maybe it did. A hotline to be used in times of crisis by the two most powerful nations on earth.

Well, there's another hotline, and from personal experience, I know it exists—to this very day. It is the direct line between my mother's lips and God's ears. If you, like I, have a praying mother or are a praying mother, you know exactly what I am talking about. Let me warn you, if my mother starts praying for you, God's hand will move. Believe me, I've watched in awe as she has turned the key to heaven for needs on this earth, especially the needs of her children. And let me clarify, I'm not talking about her biological kids, though she has spent plenty of time on her knees over us. When I speak of my mother's kids, I'm talking about a book of names. Yes, you read this right. My mother has a real book with ruled paper and lists and lists of names. Friends. Relatives. Neighbors. Even kids I've known since I was in elementary school. And when their parents died, my mother kept the prayer torch lit. She is their praying parent. Sometimes I wonder how she does it. But I never question why she prays. I've seen the results. Many years, after praying every day for someone, she'll receive a call, and a voice will say, "I knew you were praying for me all the time. I felt it." And so she keeps doing what every mother can do—even when a situation appears hopeless, even when the answer doesn't come in a day or a month or a year, even when you've prayed for fifty years and you still do not have an answer. You keep praying. And you wait. You even learn to wait patiently. And then one day when you least expect, a man comes into town. He's been walking three days on a dusty dirt road just to get to you. And the knock you hear at your front door—it's his knock. Your miracle has arrived. And his timing is perfect! How do I know? Because my mother prays!

1. How would I have gotten Jesus's attention if I had been the mother with a sick child?

2. What methods have I employed to get Jesus's attention?

3. Who are the people in my life who need me to listen to them?

4. How have I responded to them in the past?

5. How will I respond to them in the future?

6. Who are the people in my life who need me to pray for them?

7. Please add a question

Is prayer your steering wheel or your spare tire?

Corrie ten Boom, *Don't Wrestle,
Just Nestle* (1978)

Promises for Praying Mothers

Commit your way to the Lord, roll and repose each care of your load on Him, trust, lean on, rely on, and be confident also in Him and He will bring it to pass.

Psalm 37:5 AMP

She who fears the Lord has a secure fortress, and for her children it will be a refuge.

Proverbs 14:26 NIV

I will pour . . . my blessings on your children.

Isaiah 44:3 Message

For thus says the Lord: "I will contend with him who contends with you, and I will give safety to your children."

Isaiah 49:25 AMP

All your children will have God for their teacher—what a mentor for your children!

Isaiah 54:13 Message

I know whom I have believed, and am convinced that he is able to guard what I have entrusted to him for that day.

2 Timothy 1:12 NIV

Any woman who prays for any child is a praying mother.

Dorothy Valcárcel

Affirmations

Answer me when I call, O God . . . You have freed me when I was hemmed in; have mercy upon me and hear my prayer . . . The Lord listens and heeds when I call to Him . . . in peace I will both lie down and sleep, for You, Lord, alone make me dwell in safety and confident trust.

Psalm 4:1, 3, 8 AMP

When you call on me, when you come and pray to me, I'll listen. When you come looking for me, you'll find me. Yes, when you get serious about finding me and want it more than anything else, I'll make sure you won't be disappointed.

Jeremiah 29:12–13 Message

Label *(lā'bal)* n.

1. A descriptive term that identifies.

11

The Labeled Woman

And there was a woman who for eighteen years had had an
infirmity . . . she was bent completely forward and utterly
unable to straighten herself up or to look forward.

Luke 13:11 AMP

Our yearbooks had just arrived at the high school I attended.
Following the tradition of previous years, our teachers cancelled afternoon classes so we could spend time with friends
jotting down remembrances, messages that were filled with
memories of our years together.

Most of the time I found myself scribbling nondescript
notes in my friends' books, telling them to have a cool summer and ending with the pat phrase, "See ya' next year." This
worked for everyone but the seniors. Then, "Best of luck in
the future" seemed appropriate.

I was getting ready to leave my chemistry class when I
caught sight of a guy I thought was the living end, sitting in
the back of the classroom. Even though I was terribly shy, I

decided to take a deep breath and ask him to sign my year-book. I hurriedly penned a request on a piece of paper and passed my book to the girl next to me. I told her to send it to Mr. Cool. She dutifully complied with my request.

Trying not to look conspicuous I turned my head slightly to catch a sideways glance. I wanted to see if he would honor me with some treasured words. After quite a long wait I watched with expectation as he opened my yearbook and began to write.

Within a few minutes, the book was passed back across the aisle, and finally I had it in my hands.

When the noon bell rang, I couldn't wait to get to my locker. I turned page after page, searching for the words written by the guy I thought was so terrific.

I can still remember how I felt as I stared at the handwriting penned ever so neatly. Just three words: "To A Wallflower." I blinked fast as hot salty tears rolled down my cheeks. Hurrying home after school and throwing my yearbook in the garbage did nothing to ease the hurt in my heart that day.

Even now, whenever I hear the word *wallflower*, I am carried back to a moment in high school when a stinging label wounded me deeply. One word: *wallflower*. Like a neon sign flashing in my memory, it was a painful label that stuck in my mind for years.

Labeled. Classified. Branded.

Have you ever been called a name that wounded you? A name that was thrown at you like a dagger? A name you still remember? And when you hear it, you cringe at the sound?

I am certain all of us have had times in our lives when some-one called us a name we hated. You may have been on the playground at school and were the last person to be chosen for the basketball team. "Who would want her?" someone mumbled. "She's so clumsy, an uncoordinated klutz," and everybody snickered. Those words still ring in your ears. You haven't been able to forget them.

Or possibly you recall an employer embarrassing you in front of everyone at work. "You'll never amount to a hill of beans. Just look at this work. Only a dummy would do something like this." Throughout your life you have carried that label around, lacking the confidence you need because someone said you were dumb.

> Our names are labels, plainly printed on the bottled essence of our past behavior.
>
> Logan Pearsall Smith

Or if your outward appearance doesn't match the image portrayed on the cover of the latest fashion magazine, have you found yourself tagged with a name that reflects what you look like on the outside? That fat girl. That ugly woman. That wrinkled old lady.

Or if, by some misfortune, totally out of your control, you can't walk, talk, see, or hear like "normal" people, have you been called a name that reflects the perception others have of the handicap they think diminishes you?

Because of our human ability to believe the "sound bites" we pin on each other, names carry great power. My name defines me. It serves as my identity. When someone recognizes me, they call out my name and I respond. My name is a way for me to acknowledge who I am.

But names also have the tragic consequence of branding us, just like a label on a can. And when the wrong label is applied to the outside, others find it difficult to see what we are really like on the inside. While cooking supper the other night, I grabbed a can out of the pantry. The label said "Tomato Sauce." Even the size of the can was exactly the same as other cans containing identical markings. To my shock, when I opened the can, there were peaches inside. Evidently, during a recent move, the label had fallen off and I had reapplied the wrong one.

The same thing happens to you and me. We get stuck with labels that are false. They identify us only by our exterior and don't reveal who we are on the interior. I have friends whose lifelong desire is to shake some derogatory name that hangs around their neck like a dogtag, a piece of identification that has defined them simply by the weight they register on the bathroom scale or the shape of their nose or the color of their hair. They have been characterized by external features rather than internal worth. It is disastrous when we limit our vision of each other to a description that focuses on the color of our skin or nation of our birth or the way we walk or talk. But it happens all the time.

I am certain you will agree that the destruction of our identity has only been aided by a society where we become faceless lines, dots, dashes, and numbers—marks that further devalue our individuality. The government knows me as a "social security" number. My bank says I am an "account number." When I am in my car, I am a "license plate number." The catalog company I just ordered from says I am a "customer number." And somewhere in this maze of numbers and letters, I fight to grasp hold of a God, who I hope doesn't call me "910378962146784366178." From the time we are born to the day we die, we are numbered, labeled, and then finally toe-tagged.

We are dressed in camouflage that covers the reality of who we are. The result? We forget whom we were created to be.

If you have found yourself feeling trapped by a name that not only defines but diminishes you, then come meet a lady who was so boxed in by a false identity that we don't even know the name her parents gave her when she was born. We don't know where she lived or whether she got married and had children. We know only one thing about her: She had a disability. Luke 13:11 tells us she had a crooked, bent back.

The name we give to something shapes our attitude toward it.

Katherine Paterson,
Gates of Excellence

I doubt she had ever been told she was beautiful. She was never asked to enter the Miss Jerusalem pageant. Never complimented for the bright color of her eyes or the cute mole on her face. No, hers was quite a different life. She was a woman forced to stare at the ground because she could not stand erect.

Life Looking Down

Just imagine what you would do meeting a woman for the first time who was stooped over like a reed in the wind. She could not stand straight. She appeared quite the opposite of what you and I were told to do when we were kids. Ever hear the words, "Stand up straight?" I did. By the time I was fourteen years old I was nearly 5'8" and with platform shoes (remember those killers?) I could easily add two or three more inches to my height. I can still remember trying to find the flattest shoes possible when dating someone, worried I might tower over my male companion. But the bent-backed woman could not comply with the request to stand up straight.

Hers was not the lean, graceful figure of a model because she was trapped in a contorted, malformed body. She walked around town looking down, her eyes seeing nothing but dirt when the sun shown and mud when the rain fell. After eighteen long, miserable years, she began to think she was no better than the ground she was forced to observe. She couldn't even look into the faces of the townsfolk who mocked her.

"Here comes old bent-back, the crooked old stick."

Eighteen years of derision. Eighteen years of ridicule. Eighteen years of having your identity stripped away, piece by piece.

Luke says she was bound by "a spirit of infirmity" (Luke 13:11 KJV). Some biblical versions called her plague "a demon." What a way to live! On second thought, how could anyone live like this?

And while you and I will never know exactly what fiendish burden bedeviled this woman, I find it beneficial to widen our vision as to what it can mean to be "devil-possessed."

Author Linda Hollies does just that in her insightful book, *Jesus and Those Bodacious Women*. She opened my eyes to dimensions in this woman's experience that at first glance, I had not even thought about:

> There are many spirits that can cause you to walk around in a bent-over state. They might be your color, your gender, your age, your marital state, your family, or they could be abuse, injustice, resentment, oppression, despair, loneliness, your economic state, or even a physical challenge. It makes no difference what has hurt you in the past, it makes no difference how old you were when the trauma affected your life, and it makes no difference what your wealth, position, or status is. For the evil one comes to steal, kill, and destroy and each one of us is a candidate for being bent and bowed.[1]

We know this lady was bowed down, weighted by some burden that would not even allow her to lift herself up. She could not change her situation. She could not fix herself. She needed help. And maybe that is what compelled her to go to the temple, even if she went alone. Even if people stared. Even if they called her names.

Perhaps she thought the pain in her aching heart would go away inside the walls of a sacred place. Maybe she went to the temple in an attempt to find someone who would accept her—just as she was. And just maybe she heard Jesus would be there—and that was enough to get her to fight off the embarrassment and fear and go out in public. Even though we do not know exactly what drew her into the temple, we do know what kept her there. It was Jesus!

The Man Who Loves Us from the Inside Out

On this particular day there was a new face in town, a face the lady could not see. This was someone she didn't know, but someone who knew her. Someone who had a vision that saw past her deformity. A man who could get past what he saw on the outside to see what was buried on the inside.

What do you think drew Jesus to this woman? What factor in her experience touched off an explosion of compassion in his heart? To fully comprehend the empathy—yes, that is the word—Jesus had for this woman, you and I have only to look at the meaning of the word. Webster's Dictionary defines empathy as "the ability to understand another's feelings, to be able to identify with and share another's feelings or the situation they are in or the attitudes people possess toward them."

I am certain that in the temple that day there were individuals who were sympathetic to the trouble this woman faced. They were able to have sorrowful feelings toward this woman and her predicament, but, unlike Jesus, their view stopped at the outside—poor, pitiful soul. Not Jesus. He had walked in her shoes. He knew her pain for he had lived it every day since he was born.

How? Reflect for a moment on what this woman's disability had done to her. It had caused her name to be distorted. It had left her identified as nothing more than a disfigured specimen of human flesh. And if anyone understood how names and labels can destroy who we really are, Jesus did.

When he was born, the first thing people started to question were the circumstances surrounding his birth and his occupation. Mark 6:3 lifts the curtain on a drama that unfolded in Nazareth one weekend when Jesus stood up to speak. The conversation may have sounded something like this: "Hold on! Who is this guy? It's Mary's son. He's just a common laborer—nothing but a carpenter. And now he's preaching to us." And if you think saying Jesus was Mary's son was a compliment, you are mistaken. This phrase, "Jesus, son of Mary," in old desert culture meant born to a woman out-of-wedlock. Without a father's name

> Whoever degrades another degrades me.
>
> Walt Whitman,
> American poet

attached to your lineage, people concluded you were an "illegitimate child."

And then Matthew tells us that Jesus had a "party boy" reputation. He states that townsfolk called Jesus a winebibber, someone we might label a "lush." He was called a glutton, and an associate of scoundrels, like tax collectors and prostitutes. Sounds like the real cream of the crop. And if a man is known by the company he keeps, Jesus must be one of the dregs of society, the scum of the earth.

Talk about labels! Name-calling, an identity defined by exterior circumstances or behavior—oh, yes, Jesus had empathy. He understood exactly what this woman was going through, for he had been there too.

All at once the quiet of the temple service was broken by a voice that called out, "Come here. I want to meet you. You don't know me, but I know you."

The woman didn't believe Jesus was talking to her. She couldn't see his mouth form the words that were beckoning her to his side.

She felt a tap on her bent-over back.

"Hey, you. The man is talking to you."

She shrank back in fear. She didn't want to be on display, not in front of everybody, not with her crooked back. If only she could crawl in a hole and disappear. But now everyone was staring at her. She couldn't see their eyes, but she could feel them watching and looking.

A hush came over the crowd as the woman moved slowly toward Jesus. Once at his side all she could see were a pair of sandaled feet, for hers was a world of looking down. What she didn't know was that she was standing next to a man whose world was one of lifting up.

"Woman, stand up straight."

I love the way the Amplified Bible tells this story in Luke 13:12–13: "And when Jesus saw her, He called her to Him and said to her, 'Woman, you are released from your infirmity!' Then He laid His hands on her and instantly she was made straight and she recognized and thanked and praised God."

The Greek translation of the word *released* has to do with chains and irons and manacles—a prisoner's garb. So if I am released, I am set free, given my liberty. What a wonderful thought! The ball and chain that had weighed this woman down were lifted off.

Her crooked spine flexed straight to attention, and for the first time in eighteen years she was unencumbered by the physical malady that defined her. She was loosed from the prison that had bound her body and tortured her soul. Unrestricted for the first time in years, she was a free woman.

Standing straight and tall, she could look at the stranger eye to eye. She could focus on the face of the man who saw past her outside and took time to see what was on the inside. And the Bible says, "She recognized him." She knew who he was. No doubt in her mind. When you meet your liberator, you don't have to be told who he is. She understood completely!

Jesus looked into those eyes so long cast down and spoke one word: "Woman." He called her a name—not a label, not a slur, but a name that showed respect. A name with dignity, a name she had not heard in a long time, a name that gave her back her identity.

At this point in the story I imagine there was some hugging going on, as well as jumping up and down, and running about. A girl can get very excited when she knows she's been set free! A girl can dance for joy when she finally knows exactly who she is.

Our Need—His Response

Has some label obliterated your identity? Are you called a name that paints a false picture of who you really are? Do you long to lose the baggage of a name that is weighing you down, shackling your heart and binding your body?

Thankfully, you and I have been left with the example of a lady who for eighteen years lived in a faceless world, a world where her true self disappeared and a phantom self emerged, a self based on the visual image of her twisted body.

All it took for her to get her identity back was to meet the man who sees us from the inside out. He helped her realize that underneath the distorted outside was a well-defined inside outlined by a pattern of what could be—not what was.

Others might have had contempt for the woman because of what they saw. Jesus had respect for her because of what he knew. Names, labels, and slurs had not destroyed her true identity. Jesus knew that inside this woman was a heart where love could grow, where fulfillment could blossom, and where her true identity would flourish into a garden that portrayed the reality of what was there all along. All she needed to do was accept the freedom Jesus offered. As Luke wrote so beautifully the words of Jesus: "God's Spirit is on me . . . to set the burdened and battered free" (Luke 4:18 Message). And on this day, in a temple, the battered was set free!

Unlike others who see only what is "skin deep," Jesus sees us "heart deep." His view of you and me doesn't stop with the outer layer but penetrates our inner souls. His perception of me reflects the person he made me to be. "He who created you has called you by your name—because you are His" (see Isa. 43:1).

Isn't it comforting to know there is someone who knows you from the inside out and still loves you? Someone who can get past the name-calling crowd, who doesn't label us by our past faults or current problems? He never slaps a brand on us based on our outward appearance. His name for us reflects who he made us to be.

Just as he called out to the woman in the temple, he is calling out to you. Keep listening. You won't have any trouble recognizing his voice, for he will be the man who calls you by name. And it will be a name of respect, a name with dignity, the name he gave you. "See what an incredible quality of love the Father has given us, that we should be named and called the children of God! . . . Beloved, we are even here and now God's children . . ." (1 John 3:1–2 AMP).

> It seems that more than ever the compulsion today is to identify, to reduce someone to what is on the label. To identify is to control, to limit. To love is to call by name.
>
> Madeleine L'Engle,
Walking on Water

A Time for Reflection

The Labeled Woman: Woman with a Bent Back
Background Text: Luke 13:10–17

Exploration

My thoughts on being labeled . . .

1. What names have I been called that hurt me?

2. How did I feel when I was called a name I did not like?

3. What words come to mind when I describe myself?

Positive:

Negative:

4. What are five things I like about myself?
   A.
   B.
   C.
   D.
   E.

> Love yourself without condition. Love yourself through the walls of defensiveness and the darkness of your deeds. Love yourself beyond whatever you deserve for such is the love of God.
>
> Adolfo Quezada, *Loving Yourself for God's Sake*

Inspiration

> Whoever comes to me, I will never drive away.
>
> John 6:37 NIV

Did you ever wonder why Jesus seemed drawn to people who had been driven away by others? When someone was called an inflammatory or degrading name, Jesus showed them great compassion. The worse the case, the kinder his treatment.

People with leprosy, who had to scream out the word *unclean*, were even touched by Jesus, an unheard-of response at that time. The names they were called because of their diseased bodies didn't hinder his response to their hurting hearts. And it should not stop us from responding to people with AIDS or any other problem that causes individuals to feel labeled and then ostracized.

It is this empathy and understanding that led Jesus into the life of a woman who had been branded like an animal and scarred for life. But rather than shove her away as others had, Jesus invited her to his side. He invited her to "Come as you are."

In the inspirational book *Then Sings My Soul*, author Robert J. Morgan tells the historical and biographical stories behind the authorship of some of the world's most famous hymns.

Of all the songs written, the invitational hymn "Just As I Am" invokes memories of televised Billy Graham Crusades, ending with an altar call where thousands of individuals make their way down the aisles of an arena, and portrays the loving acceptance Jesus offers to the unwanted, the castoffs, the labeled.

Robert J. Morgan writes so touchingly about the author of this moving song:

> She was an embittered woman, Charlotte Elliott of Brighton, England. Her health was broken, and her disability had hardened her. "If God loved me," she muttered, "He would not have treated me this way." Hoping to help her, a Swiss minister, Dr. Cesar Malan, visited the Elliotts on May 9, 1822. Over dinner, Charlotte lost her temper and railed against God and family in a violent outburst. Her embarrassed family left the room, and Dr. Malan was left alone with her.
>
> "You are tired of yourself, aren't you?" he asked. "You are holding to your hate and anger because you have nothing else in the world to cling to. Consequently, you have become sour, bitter, and resentful."
>
> "What is your cure?" asked Charlotte.
>
> "The faith you are trying to despise."
>
> As they talked, Charlotte softened. "If I wanted to become a Christian and to share the peace and joy you possess," she finally asked, "what would I do?"

"You would give yourself to God just as you are now, with your fightings and fears, hates and loves, pride and shame."

"I would come to God just as I am? Is that right?"

Charlotte did come to Jesus just as she was, and her heart was changed that day. As time passed she found and claimed John 6:37 as a special verse for her: "He who comes to me I will by no means cast out."

Years later, her brother, Rev. Henry Elliott, was raising funds for England. The leaflet said: *Sold for the Benefit of St. Margaret's Hall, Brighton: Him That Cometh to Me I Will No Wise Cast Out*. Underneath was Charlotte's poem— which has since become the most famous invitational hymn in history.

Charlotte lived to be 82 and wrote about 150 hymns, though she never enjoyed good health. As her loved ones sifted through her papers after her death, they found over a thousand letters she had kept in which people expressed their gratitude for the way this hymn had touched their lives.[2]

Just like Charlotte, the bent-over woman came to Jesus just as she was. She accepted his gracious invitation, "Come." And his invitation is still open to you and me. He invites us to "Come as you are." Broken. Bruised. And, yes, bent over with our burdens.

1. If I had met Jesus in the temple and he called me to his side, how would I have reacted?

2. How did Jesus respond to the "labels" people placed on him? (Luke 7:34–35; Matt. 11:19; John 6:41–44).

3. Where did Jesus turn for affirmation? (John 3:17 NIV/ Message).

> My feeling is that there is nothing in life but refraining from hurting others, and comforting those that are sad.
>
> Olive Schreiner, *The Letters of Olive Schreiner*

Affirmation

What marvelous love the Father has extended to us! Just look at it—we're called children of God! That's who we really are.

1 John 3:1–2 Message

Hopeless *(hōp'l´ls) adj.*
1. Having no hope: despairing.
2. Having no possibility of solution.

12

The Hopeless Woman

Soon afterward Jesus went to a town called Nain, and His disciples and a great throng accompanied Him. Just as He drew near the gate of the town, behold, a man who had died was being carried out, the only son of his mother, and she was a widow; and a large gathering from the town was accompanying her. And when the Lord saw her, He had compassion on her and said to her, "Do not weep."

Luke 7:11–13 AMP

There are days we never forget: a wedding day, the day a child is born—and the day someone we love dies.

It was 10:06 p.m. on May 26, 1987. The ring of the phone broke the evening silence. It was my mother. I had anticipated her call. My parents were traveling and every night, upon arriving at the hotel, they called me just to say they were safe.

But this time something seemed wrong. My mother's voice cracked as she spoke.

"Daddy had a heart attack."

I couldn't believe what I heard. The day before I had watched my father exercise for over an hour on his Nordic Trak machine. Fifteen minutes on that piece of equipment wore me out, but not Daddy. He barely broke a sweat.

"How is he?" I asked, never imagining he would be anything but fine.

Silence. Then words I will never forget: "Dorothy, Daddy is dead."

My legs gave way. I slid down on the floor. This must be a bad dream. I hoped it was. I did not want to believe my dad was dead. But soon reality struck.

The days that followed were a blur—finding a grave plot, buying a casket, preparing for a funeral. I had not planned for this to happen. No one in our family had. A sudden catastrophic event had snatched my father away.

I am not certain how we got through the first few days after Daddy's death. Thankfully, there were family members around to lend comfort. Well-meaning friends tried to provide solace by telling me, "Time heals everything."

I did not say the words out loud, but I wanted to tell them to keep their remarks to themselves. Time was not the healer I wanted. At that moment, I wanted my father back, alive.

As the days passed, everyone had to get on with life, and soon those of us who loved my dad most were left to face the grief and loneliness that accompany the loss of a dear one.

Eventually, the initial shock turned to a nagging ache. Every Christmas the vacant spot where Daddy used to sit at the holiday table served to underline his absence.

Special dates like his birthday and my parents' wedding anniversary came and went with visits to his grave, visits that reminded me how much he was missed. There was a void in our family, an empty place no one else could fill. Nineteen years later I still experience a stabbing pain when I pass a cemetery and see a fresh spray of flowers lying on the grass. It brings back memories of the sorrow I felt standing next to my own father's grave.

Grieving. Dying. Death.

Have you lost someone you've loved? Was it a child too young to be taken? A spouse with whom you shared a lifetime of love and devotion? Maybe it was a trusted friend or favorite relative.

Death. I do not even like to say the word. It is so painful. So irrevocable. So final. It steals into our lives without warning, robbing us of friendships and snatching away our loved ones. It leaves us alone and brokenhearted.

Death. The great common denominator. Striking rich and poor. Young and old. Male and female. And whether the person we love dies without warning or lingers with a debilitating illness, when death comes the loss is devastating. How we wish we could turn back the clock, making certain no words were left unsaid and no deeds undone.

Just a few days ago I was visiting a local hospice and overheard a conversation between two elderly couples. "It seems everyone I know has lost someone recently," sighed one of the men. "Life is so fragile." Perhaps you can relate to his sentiment.

But there is another destructive consequence when death enters our lives. Death often serves as an extinguisher, blowing out the fire of hope that burns within our hearts.

When a loved one is ill, we hope for the best. We hope the doctors will find a cure. We hope a miracle will happen. We have even coined a phrase for the way we feel: as long as there is life, there is hope.

Yet when death rushes in, hope flees a casualty of our grief, a result of the pain we are experiencing. "Death is the greatest evil," wrote British essayist William Hazlitt, "because it cuts

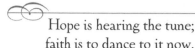

Hope is hearing the tune;
faith is to dance to it now.

Ruben Alves

off hope." In Hebrew, "death" means "separation from God." That most definitely is cutting off hope, isn't it?

If you have felt the wrenching pain that accompanies the death of someone you love, and if the fire of hope in your heart is only a mere flicker, then come take a walk with me to the city gate in a town called Nain, where death has claimed another victim. But today there's going to be a collision. At last—death will meet its match.

The Queen of Tissue

She could not believe what the doctors told her. They said her husband would die. He was too young and they had plans. They had a child to raise. She never thought she would be handling things alone, but the doctors were right. Her husband passed away, and now she was a single mom raising a son.

Grief consumed her days, fear her nights. It was difficult to focus. Each day she went through the motions of getting up, getting dressed, and preparing breakfast. It was a dull routine, but a routine she could handle.

She tried to hide her tears from her son, for he also missed his dad. The last thing she wanted to do was upset his world any more than it had been. But just as life was beginning to get back to normal, disaster struck again. Her boy became sick and the unthinkable happened: the widow's only child also died.

Now the house was empty. Friends came around to try and cheer her up, but their efforts were useless. Why should she even get up in the morning? Grab another hankie.

The tears were flowing—again. When her husband died she had forced herself to survive for her son's sake. Now with her boy gone, life was not worth living. All hope was gone.

170

The sound of wailing outside her door served as an abrupt reminder that she must leave with the mourners. They were going to follow the makeshift stretcher bearing the body of her dead child.

It was a sad, slow-moving procession that headed down the dusty street toward the city gate to the burial grounds outside the city. But all at once the funeral cortege stopped.

On this particular day, if you were to read the evening newspaper in Nain, the headline would go something like this: *Party Crowd Runs into Pallbearers.*

The Man Who Puts Hope in Your Heart

This was a great day for Jesus. The crippled could walk. The dumb could speak. The deaf could hear. The blind could see. As the noisy multitude surrounding Jesus moved toward the city of Nain, coming in the opposite direction was a weeping crowd of townsfolk. It looked as though the entire community had turned out to support a distraught widow who had lost her only child (see Luke 7:11–13).

There were two groups of people going in opposite directions, acting in two different ways: the party crowd and the pallbearers, running headlong into each other, and standing right in between them was Jesus. Life on one side—death on the other. Hope was fueling the fire on one side, while hopelessness was blowing out the fire on the other.

Jesus began to move toward the funeral bier and the body of a lifeless boy. His voice broke the silence of the moment.

"Young man, I say to you, arise" (Luke 7:14 AMP). That was all. And what happened? "The man who was dead sat up and began to speak." But the story isn't over. This is the part I love the most. Luke wrote, "And Jesus gave him back to his mother" (Luke 7:15 AMP). Needless to say, that one act brought an abrupt halt to the funeral.

Life and death had come face-to-face. The funeral procession would join the party crowd. When Jesus came to town he didn't just give a widow back the son she needed, he rekindled the fire of hope in her heart—and in your heart and mine.

Our Need—His Response

If the pain of losing a dear one hangs over you like a dark cloud, making each day difficult to face, the Man who brought hope to a grieving widow wants to put hope back in your heart.

On that day in Nain, Jesus lit a candle of hope in the heart of every mom, every dad, every brother, and every sister who ever lived. When he gave a hopeless widow back her son, he sent you a message that he will give you back your loved one as well. Jesus wants hope to serve as our magnifying glass, allowing us to see clearly when the pain of life blurs reality beyond recognition.

When I was growing up, our family spent many summers camping at Greer in the White Mountains of Arizona. Every day in the afternoon, clouds would roll in and there would be a brief downpour. We called it a "cloudburst." Rain would fall, fast and hard, and we would run for cover in our tent where we were protected from the storm.

As you and I are buffeted by the storm of losing someone we love, hope serves as our covering, a tent of protection. Hope keeps us believing we will receive what we have been promised.

"Hope appears to be anti-human," wrote Patrick Henry in the *Ironic Christian's Companion*. He continues by offering this view. "Hope may seem to some like the expectation of pie in the sky when we die, so that the everyday world with its human constituents and its intractable problems dwindles into insignificance. But hope is not blind or insensitive."[1]

Hope feeds my soul as bread feeds my body. It nourishes me and gives me the strength to see past the harsh realities of life. Author Norman Wright in his book *Chosen for Blessing* offers this perspective: "Hope is a choice. When we have hope, some of the pain of a circumstance is less because we are looking beyond the situation to what will happen in the future." [2]

When the sting of death pierces your heart, you can find comfort in these words: "He will swallow up death in victory— He will abolish death forever; and the Lord God will wipe away tears from off all faces . . ." (Isa. 25:8 AMP).

This assurance transforms the hopeless into the hopeful. Death will not win. Jesus made sure of it!

> Death be not proud, though some have called thee
> mighty and dreadful, for, thou art not so,
> For, those, whom thou think'st, thou dost overthrow,
> Die not, poor death, nor yet canst thou kill me. . . .
> One short sleep past, we wake eternally,
> And death shall be no more; death, thou shalt die.

John Donne, *Divine Poems X*, public domain

A Time for Reflection

The Hopeless Woman: Widow of Nain
Background Text: Luke 7:11–17

Exploration

My thoughts on feeling hopeless . . .

1. Was there an event in my life that left me feeling completely hopeless?

2. What was that event?

3. If I have ever felt hopeless over the death of a loved one, who was it?

4. What made that loss so difficult to bear?

> Why art thou cast down, O my soul? And why art thou disquieted in me? Hope thou in God: for I shall yet praise him for the help of his contenance.
>
> Psalm 42:5 KJV

Inspiration

When my grandmother was twelve years old, her father, a marine engineer, left on a sailing trip one morning and never returned. Several months after the disappearance of the ship he was on, an empty life preserver was found floating in the Atlantic Ocean. For my grandmother, as well as all the other family members whose loved ones served aboard this vessel, it was a devastating loss.

As I grew older, there was one thing about my grandma I could never understand. She never cried. No matter how sad the event—even at funerals—grandma never shed a tear. One day at the age when you have more boldness than brains, I went into my grandma's office where she was busy typing and I said with all my youthful bluntness, "Grandma, why don't you ever cry?"

She looked at me and said, "Well, Dorothy, long ago when I was about your age and my father died, I found out that tears never fix anything." I'll never forget those words. I thought long and hard about what my grandma said for many years—even believing, myself, that shedding tears over anything was a waste of time.

One day, after a particularly hurtful end to a very painful

> Hope arouses as nothing else can arouse, a passion for the possible.
>
> William Sloan Coffin

174

relationship, I happened to be visiting Grandma. As we talked about the situation that to me was so traumatic, I began to cry. Not a little trickle of water. These weren't small droplets on my cheeks. No, this was

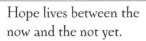

Hope lives between the now and the not yet.

Barry Johnson,
Choosing Hope

something unusual. I was crying huge crocodile tears. An unstoppable flood covered my face, and loud, wailing howls came out of my mouth. To my complete surprise, I looked up and saw tears rolling down the soft, wrinkled face of my dear grandmother.

She got up from where she was sitting and went into her bedroom and got the old, very used Bible that was on a table beside her bed and read me these words: "Thou tellest my wanderings; put thou my tears into thy bottle; are they not in thy book?" (Ps. 56:8 KJV).

Grandma took my hands and said, "Dearie, God has every one of your tears and mine in the bottle of his remembrance." And this is when I found out where all my grandma's tears were—held in loving hands in a beautiful place where God never forgets the pain that has crushed our dreams and broken our hearts.

As the Message states, "You've kept track of my every toss and turn through the sleepless nights, each tear entered in your ledger, each ache written in your book" (Ps. 56:8). God keeps a complete record. A written document. A remembrance of the tears that have filled our eyes and rolled down our cheeks.

This comforting thought took on a whole new meaning for me when I read Dr. Larry Dossey's recent thought-provoking book, *The Extraordinary Healing Power of Ordinary Things*. One chapter deals specifically with the healing power of tears. Dr. Dossey notes that throughout ancient history, it was a sign of love and caring to collect tears in "bottlelike containers called lachrymatories."[3]

175

But this isn't all I learned. Scientists have found that "tears contain more than thirty times the amount of manganese found in the blood. This suggests that tears may function to rid the body of certain toxins. Indeed, in seabirds such as cormorants and albatrosses, tear glands seem to serve this purpose; they are more powerful than the birds' kidneys in ridding the body of toxic levels of salt."[4]

As I thought about the potential for physical cleansing as we release tears, I remembered words written by the apostle John in Revelation where God assures us that in one of the most compassionate acts of love ever recorded in the Scriptures, he will "wipe every tear from our eyes. Death will be gone for good—tears gone, crying gone, pain gone." God isn't going to find some stand-in to perform this task. He wants to end the suffering himself. And so with the gentle hands of a loving Father, he will reach over and wipe from your face those droplets of water that on earth have served to help purify our bodies from the toxins caused by pain, grief, heartbreak, and sadness.

> The longest day must have its close, the gloomiest night will wear to a morning.
>
> Harriet Beecher Stowe, *Uncle Tom's Cabin*

It is no wonder our heavenly Father gives us his word when he says that tears will be a thing of the past. It is because in heaven, God is making "everything new." And then he tells us we can count on his word. "Write it all down—each word is dependable and accurate" (Rev. 21:4 Message).

No need for tears because a day is coming when nothing will cause tears. No pain. No sadness. No heartache.

And that, my dear friend, is enough good news to nourish the seed of hope God has planted in our hearts.

1. How would I have felt if I had been a witness to the events in Nain?

176

2. What if I were a part of the party crowd?

3. What if I had been in the funeral procession?

4. When I have felt completely hopeless, how was hope rekindled in my heart?

5. How can I live a more hopeful life now?

> I still miss those I loved who are no longer with me but I find I am grateful for having loved them. The gratitude has finally conquered the loss.
>
> Rita Mae Brown

> In many cases, people who've become aware of their mortality find that they've gained the freedom to live. They are seized with an appreciation for the present: every day is my best day; this is my life; I'm not going to have this moment again. They spend more time with the things and people they love and less time on people and pastimes that don't offer love or joy. This seems like such a simple thought—shouldn't we all spend our lives that way?—But we tend not to make those kinds of choices until somebody says, "You have twelve months to live."
>
> Bernie Siegel, *Handbook for the Soul*

Affirmation

> Blessed is the [woman] who believes in, trusts in, and relies on the Lord, and whose hope and confidence the Lord is.
>
> Jeremiah 17:7 AMP

Guilty *(gŭl′tē)* adj.

1. *Remorseful awareness of having done something wrong.*

13

The Guilty Woman

But the Scribes and Pharisees brought to him a woman who had been caught in adultery. They made her stand in front, and then said to him, "Now, master, this woman has been caught in adultery, in the very act. According to the Law, Moses commanded us to stone such women to death. Now, what do you say about her?"

John 8:3–5 Phillips

If you met her you would love her—my friend Mary.

She is warm, fun-loving, compassionate, and generous to a fault. I have rarely heard her complain about anything—a trait she inherited from her mother. When I met Mary over thirty years ago, I knew she would be a friend for life.

A few minutes with this bubbly wonder and you would think Mary's life was a bed of roses and always had been. But over the years, as I have gotten to know her better, I have found that life hasn't always been easy for Mary.

> Guilt is a rope that wears thin.
>
> Ayn Rand

When she was sixteen her father died. Then, just ninety days before Mary's graduation from high school, her brother, a policeman, was shot one hour after leaving work. His injuries left him paralyzed and unable to do his job. Things became so tough that Mary's mom ended up selling her engagement and wedding rings for $400 (a great deal at that time) to help her son face a long, uphill physical battle. With rising debt, the family savings earmarked for Mary's nursing education were used to pay her brother's medical expenses. So, instead of attending college, Mary took the first job she could find and quickly settled into her work, thankful she was able to help her widowed mother with mounting bills. As time went by, the owner of the company gave her more responsibility. Soon she was manager of the entire office.

Not long after beginning her employment, Mary and her boss began to spend more time together. He was going through a divorce, and sharing the company of a young woman became the highlight of his week. Although he was more than twice Mary's age, their shared interests and their work balanced any differences caused by age.

It was not long before the gentleman's divorce was final, and a year later Mary and her companion eloped, looking forward to a future together. What Mary was not prepared for was the vitriolic outpouring directed her way, especially from friends who were incensed by the turn of events and did not like what they saw. Furthermore, at the time these events took place, it raised eyebrows when a young woman was having a relationship with an older, newly divorced man.

No sooner was Mary married than the pastor of her church called. "Some people feel very uncomfortable with this situation," he told her. "You can avoid a lot of trouble if you will send me a letter requesting your name be deleted from our membership records."

Mary was crushed. The last thing she wanted to do was cause a problem, so she honored the pastor's request.

However, several weeks later, when Mary arrived at the front door for the weekly service, she was still met by a "welcoming" committee who informed her in no uncertain terms, "Your kind is not wanted here. I thought we made it clear. Don't come back."

Harsh story, you may be thinking. I agree wholeheartedly. Thankfully, not all the people in Mary's church were as cruel to her as a few.

And while her experience is not an indictment on the way "religious folk" treat one another, this example is appropriate because it points out what happens when we let our piety and prejudice override our compassion and concern.

Guilty. Liable. Sinful.

Like Mary, have you ever been held up for public condemnation because of something you did? Your friends scattered, and your foes gloated. You felt like everyone was gossiping about you, watching you, and criticizing you.

I am certain we can all recall times in our lives when we did something we wished we had not. The mistake may have been so large it has affected the rest of your life. You may even find yourself defined by your error. Accusing fingers are pointed in your direction, and you hear the whispers: "Remember what she did?"

How you wish you could take back that moment of poor judgment or raw passion or youthful foolishness! You know you would never make the same mistake again. Over and over you ask yourself, "How could I have been so stupid?"

If you have found yourself cringing at the memory of mistakes you have made, then I know someone you need to meet—a girl who really messed up. But when she botched up her life, she did it in front of the whole town. And just like my friend Mary, the people who were on her case first were religious folk. Rather than using their hands to lift this fallen girl up, they used them to point and pick up stones!

Caught in the Act

In order to create a proper mental picture of this drama, I want to start at the beginning, the way the disciple John chronicled the events in the New Testament (see John 8:1–11).

Jesus had been on the Mount of Olives during the night, a favorite retreat where he spent time in meditation and prayer.

As John tells the story, "Early in the morning he came again into the temple, and all the people came unto him; and he sat down, and taught them" (John 8:2 KJV).

I don't know exactly what the word *all* means. My super thesaurus says, "totality, everything, entirety." And the Greek translation expands the definition further by offering this meaning, "as many as." Let's just say that as many people as were at the temple joined Jesus for a scriptural lesson that day. A peaceful time of quiet thought and reflection. Then, all of a sudden, the scribes and Pharisees arrived on the scene and brought a woman caught in adultery and dumped her at Jesus's feet.

The Pharisees were men who were deeply concerned about following the laws of Moses down to the tiniest detail. They were often businessmen and merchants, and since most of them did not have formal educational training in "the interpretation of the law," they brought along the learned scribes to back up their claims.

At that moment, they were only using this "fallen" woman to try to back Jesus into a corner. Harkening back to the words of Moses, they reminded Jesus, "The man that committeth adultery with his neighbor's wife, the adulterer and the adulteress shall surely be put to death" (Lev. 20:10). There it was in black and white—at least, this was what this holy group of men thought. But the scene begs this question: Where was the man who had been the other half of this lustful pair? Evidently, in their haste to point a critical finger, the woman got all the blame. Not the first time some poor girl was left to carry the consequences of a mistake that required the involvement of two people.

> Know all and you will pardon all.
>
> Thomas à Kempis

From this girl's point of view, she had done wrong. She was caught with another woman's husband. She knew better. But when Mr. Handsome came to her door, she could not resist him. She was lonely that day. How she wished for someone who would hold her. And there he was—smiling, warm, appealing.

His soft voice whispered in her ear, "You don't know how much I have missed you. All I could do the past few days was think about you. I wanted to smell your perfume, touch your hair, and hold you in my arms."

How could she say no? With talk like that the girl took a tumble, falling willingly for this man's charm and his line.

Make no mistake, she was not an innocent victim. She was an adult. She knew he belonged to someone else, but in a moment of weakness nothing else mattered except the two of them. Their wants. Their needs. Their desires. If there were consequences to their behavior, they would deal with them at a later date. Tonight they were going to do what they wanted.

But when the morning light pierced the bedroom windows, the previous night's pleasure became a faded memory. It was time to face the day and the music. Unfortunately, the tune playing outside her window was not melodic. It was the thundering of angry voices, followed by persistent banging on her front door. The detectives were on her doorstep. She had been caught in the act, and there was no way of escape.

"We caught you. What do you have to say for yourself now?"

And so, in front of "all" the people at the temple, the quietness of the morning was disrupted by a group of "Holy Men" demanding justice. The rule of law must be obeyed or anarchy would reign.

No time to tend to their businesses—especially when these voyeurs could pursue a victim of sexual impropriety. It wasn't enough to humiliate this woman in front of everybody—these guys wanted her dead. Stoned until her last gasp.

With great pomp, the purity patrol attempted to back Jesus into a corner by asking, "What sayest thou?" In other words, "Are you going to agree with Moses, or are you going to break the law too?"

The Man Who Forgives and Forgets

Jesus took a moment to quiet the noisy crowd. Then, with deliberate strokes he began writing in the sand, very likely carving a record of the sins of these very men in the dirt— emblazoned for everyone to see.

The people pressed toward Jesus, hoping to catch a glimpse of the words. As the crowd pushed forward, the accusers fell backward, slinking into the temple hallways, embarrassed when the curtain was lifted and their hidden lives were placed on public display. For all we know one of those very men may have been the other half of this love match. And now, with their own secrets revealed, these paragons of piety had no choice but to disappear.

And then there were two. Jesus and a woman.

"Where are the tattletales?" he asked.

> If you judge people, you have no time to love them.
>
> Mother Teresa

The frightened woman was so petrified she had not yet lifted her head. But when she did, imagine her shock to see she was alone with the Man who held her fate in his hands.

"Is there anyone condemning you now?"

She had to think a minute. Her accusers had left. The crowd was not saying anything. They could not condemn her. They had not witnessed her sexual act, as had the men who brought the original complaint. Now Jesus had said he did not condemn her, either.

That left just one person, the toughest critic of all. This woman was the only one left to condemn herself for the mistakes she had made. She had to live with her guilt. She had to face the memory of her failures.

And Jesus knew this. So he gave her some advice on how to live above the guilt of a misspent past. He asked the woman to do one thing: "Forgive yourself. Don't live in the past. Start fresh. Go, and live a new life."

It was a simple request to a guilty woman, three steps to help her live above the record of past failures.

Step One: Let me take care of your accusers. Let me handle the rumors. Leave the gossips to me.

Step Two: I do not accuse you. My forgiveness is a gift. He promised, "My compassion is on its way to you. I'll stamp out your wrongdoing, I'll sink your sins to the bottom of the ocean" (see Mic. 7:19).

Step Three: Forgive yourself. I have forgiven and forgotten your past—now I ask you to do the same. As the Message so beautifully reflects in the book of Micah, "You held tight to my lifeline. You never let me tumble over the edge into nothing. But my sins you let go of, threw them over your shoulder—good riddance!" (Isa. 38:16 Message).

She was a guilty woman, living with the consequences of her behavior. On the chalkboard of her life was a record of every error, written clearly for everyone to see.

Jesus did not want her to let the memory of her past destroy the promise of her future, so he came along with a great big eraser and wiped the board clean. Not a mark was left. She started over—perfect.

Our Need—His Response

Are you trying to stitch together the tattered pieces of your life? Are you attempting to right the wrongs, mend the fences, repair what is broken? But, sadly, you keep running into people who take great delight in reminding you of your past failings, holding up the record of your life with a list of every mistake you have ever made. You feel the accusing glares. You hear the muted whispers. You see the pointing fingers. And if others won't forgive you, what hope do you have of forgiving yourself? If I am describing the way you feel, these words of Henry Ward Beecher will encourage you: "Forgiveness ought to be like a cancelled note—torn in two and burned up so that it can never be shown against one." Can you tear up the mistakes in your past? Will you let the fire of Jesus's love burn up the memories of errors you have made? Ezekiel 33:15–16 is a beautiful promise: "None of [her] wrongs that [she] committed shall be mentioned." Gone. Wiped away. Not just forgiven, but forgotten, as well.

If you find yourself tormented by past mistakes or today's failure, then go to the Man with the eraser in his hand. My friend Mary did. And soon she was coming to the rescue of some of the very people who had been so cruel to her. Isn't it amazing what happens when we not only forgive but, instead of seeking revenge, we choose to love?

If your past is painful and your future appears daunting, look to Jesus. He is standing in front of you. In one hand he holds an eraser, in the other a clean slate. At the top of the board is a name; it is yours.

There is tremendous relief in knowing that His love to me is utterly realistic, based at every point on prior knowledge of the worst about me, so that no discovery now can disillusion Him about me, in the way I am so often disillusioned about myself, and quench His determination to bless me.

J. I. Packer, *Knowing God*

I've wiped the slate of all your wrongdoings. There's nothing left of your sins. Come back to me, come back. I've redeemed you.

Isaiah 44:22 Message

I have swept away your offenses like a cloud, your sins like the morning mist. Return to me, for I have redeemed you.

Isaiah 44:22 NIV

A Time for Reflection

The Guilty Woman: A Woman Caught in Adultery
Background Text: John 8:1–20

Exploration

My thoughts on feeling guilty . . .

1. What mistakes haunt my memory?

2. What have others said about my mistakes?

   How did their responses make me feel?

3. What mistakes am I condemning myself for?

4. Who has suffered by my mistakes?
   What have I done to alleviate their pain?

As far as the east is from the west, so far has He removed our transgressions from us.

Psalm 103:12 NKJV

Inspiration

There is an old-time story told about two brothers who both
chose to take destructive paths in their lives. After being repeatedly caught for acts of sheep stealing, the presiding judge
in their case passed down a sentence that required both brothers to have the brand "ST"—"Sheep Thief"—placed on their
foreheads. One brother, unable to live above the disgrace and
shame that accompanied such a visible punishment, left town
never to be heard from again.

The other brother took a different road. He began to make
restitution to all the people he had stolen sheep from, and
after years of being recognized as one of his town's most
beloved citizens, a newcomer in the village inquired as to the
meaning of the "ST" mark on the man's forehead. Several
citizens of the community shook their heads, saying they
couldn't remember what the brand meant, but they thought
it stood for "Saint." Jesus promises, "I will write on [her] my
new name" (Rev. 3:12 NIV). The past is forgotten. We get a
fresh start with a new heart and a new name.

I'll give you a new heart, put a new spirit in you. I'll remove
the stone heart from your body and replace it with a heart
that's God-willed, not self-willed.

Ezekiel 36:26 Message

And then take on an entirely new way of life—a God-fashioned
life, a life renewed from the inside.

Ephesians 4:24 Message

1. What will it take for me to accept forgiveness from the
   Man with the eraser?

188

2. Whom do I need to forgive?
   What steps can I take to do so?

3. What will it take for me to forgive myself for the mistakes I have made?

> He spoke to her: "I forgive your sins."
>
> Luke 7:48 Message

Affirmations

> Count yourself lucky, how happy you must be—you get a fresh start, your slate's wiped clean.
>
> Psalm 32:1 Message

> Blessed is [she] whose transgressions are forgiven, whose sins are covered.
>
> Psalm 32:1 NIV

Stressed *(strĕs'd)*

1. Mental, emotional, or physical tension.

2. Strain or distress.

14

The Stressed Woman

Jesus came to a village and a woman called Martha welcomed him to her house. She had a sister by the name of Mary who settled down at the Lord's feet and was listening to what he said. But Martha was very worried about her elaborate preparations and she burst in, saying, "Lord, don't you mind that my sister has left me to do everything by myself? Tell her to come and help me!" But the Lord answered her, "Martha, my dear, you are worried and bothered about providing so many things. Only one thing is really needed."

Luke 10:38–42 Phillips

I come from a long line of busybodies.

No, I'm not talking about individuals who stick their noses into other people's business. I am referring to bodies that are in constant motion. You may know the type—people who can't sit down for a minute to relax.

My grandmother Myrtle Pohle was the first family member to carry the "perpetual motion" gene. People who have this

> There is a big difference between having many choices and making a choice. Making a choice—declaring what is essential—creates a framework for a life that eliminates many choices but gives meaning to the things that remain. This may mean I have to learn to set boundaries. I will have to make choices. And I will have to say no.
>
> Sue Bender, *Plain and Simple,* Patch #9

genetic trait can be identified by their motto: "Idle hands are the Devil's workshop." Believe me, this phrase was Grandma's mantra. And she took the admonition seriously.

Every summer, when my sister and I arrived at Grandma's for "vacation," we felt as though we had enlisted in the army and were in boot camp. To say our time was structured would be an understatement. We were controlled by the General Patton of "Godly Activity," and in this woman's army there was no time for goofing off.

When Grandma awoke in the morning, she jumped out of bed prepared to work. She kept a list, close at hand, that detailed her daily activities. This way she knew exactly when she had a spare moment to squeeze in some other endeavor.

At 6:00 a.m. or before, you could hear pots clanking in the kitchen. The dining room table was set by 6:30, and by 7:30 breakfast was over for the day. If you hadn't gotten up yet, you were on your own. Grandma was long gone. She had things to do, people to see, and places to go.

The lights never went out at night until at least 11:00 p.m. And in between those times you could find Grandma taking food to the sick, feeding lunch and dinner to everybody and anybody who happened to stop at her house, providing beds for the weary, giving money to the destitute, counseling the troubled, and substituting as mother to over twenty foster children. Oh, I almost forgot. She also had a job as a medical records librarian and raised three children of her own while assisting my grandfather, who was a physician in a small town.

If you get high marks for virtuous activity, Grandma would be ready for sainthood. Her front door always had someone coming in, and her back door always had a smiling face and full stomach going out. We nicknamed her house "Grand Central Station." And that name fit!

This hum of activity wasn't limited to the inside of Grandma's house. It extended to her car, too. In the evening, if Grandpa invited us to go for a ride in the balmy Arizona evening, Grandma would break away from her activities to come along, but only if she could do something "constructive." And in her case, it meant grabbing a knitting bag.

I have no idea how many sweaters and afghans Grandma managed to complete on those drives. Let's just say every relative, friend, and neighbor benefited from her talent. Thankfully, there were no reports of stabbings in our family due to knitting needles flying around the car.

Having grown up in this environment where godliness was a virtue associated with your work ethic, it doesn't take a genius to figure out that my mother, the daughter of Mrs. Workaholic, inherited the same motion gene that Grandma had.

My mom succeeds at anything she does. And believe me, she does a lot. She is a phenomenal cook, gracious hostess, talented musician, accomplished businesswoman, loving mom, and great wife. If something needs to get done, give it to my mother. Not only will the task

What a circus act we women perform every day of our lives. It puts the trapeze artist to shame. Look at us. We run a tight rope daily, balancing a pile of books on the head. Babycarriage, parasol, kitchen chair, still under control. Steady now! This is not the life of simplicity but the life of multiplicity that the wise men warn us of. It leads not to unification but to fragmentation. It does not bring grace; it destroys the soul.

Anne Morrow Lindbergh,
Gift from the Sea

193

be done right, it will be done quickly. If you look in your dictionary under the definition of *organized*, you will find a picture of my mother.

I have never walked into her home, even unexpectedly, when I could not have eaten off the floor. It doesn't matter how much company has visited, her house is always neat and clean. There is always food in the refrigerator just in case someone drops by and is hungry. She has handled her life with the poise of a queen while raising a family and working full-time.

Don't get me wrong. I am not critical of my family tree. I am overwhelmed by it. But I have come to the conclusion my genes don't carry the same DNA as my grandmother and mother.

I don't possess their energy. I can't keep up with them. I've tried, only to find myself panting like a dog running behind a speeding fire truck. I'm afraid their legacy is going to have to skip a generation.

The fact is, in my unsuccessful pursuit to be the next in our family lineage to wear the crown of efficiency, I have found myself stressed out and burned up. When you light a candle at both ends, it burns twice as fast.

Stressed-out. Harried. Overworked.

So how was your day? Are you trying to cram too much into twenty-four hours? Do your feet ache? Are your nerves frayed? Are your eyelids drooping?

You would think with all the time-saving gadgets that have been invented we would have more time to just kick up our feet and relax. But if you are like me, even your supposed spare moments end up getting filled to the brim with activity.

Just this past week I found myself frustrated by circumstances associated with electronic wizardry designed to save time. Someone came to the front door and impatiently began ringing the bell. At the same time the phone rang and my fax machine, which had run out of paper, started beeping. If that weren't enough, my pager went off.

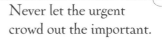

Never let the urgent crowd out the important.

Kelly Catlin Walker

At that moment I wanted to throw several pieces of equipment in the garbage. To quote my niece Aimee, "It's too much already!"

Sometimes I think Thoreau had it right when he penned these words: "Our life is frittered away by detail. Simplicity. Simplicity. Simplicity. I say, let our affairs be as two or three, and not a hundred or a thousand."

But what do I do? Instead of simplifying my life, I complicate it by filling every waking minute with activities I perceive worthwhile. Every day is a frenzy, and by evening, I am lucky if I can keep my eyes open long enough to find my way to bed.

I know I am not alone feeling overwhelmed by my daily routine. We're probably running down the same road together. Doctors now have a name for what we busy women suffer from. They call it the "Hurried Woman Syndrome." Not surprisingly, the two chief symptoms of this "disease" are fatigue and moodiness. And what do the experts offer as a cure for this affliction? One therapist proposed this solution: "Get organized."

Nice thought, but I've found organization won't cure me. When your plate is filled to overflowing you can try as hard as you want to reorganize things, but if there's too much on the plate you don't solve your problem by moving everything around!

In her book *A Place Called Simplicity*, author Claire Cloninger offered insight into the challenges we face as we try to get our lives in order. "So often we have the mistaken idea that the more things and activities and relationships we have in our lives, the more meaningful our lives will be. Ironically, the converse is often true. An overabundance of commitments and involvements actually tires us and drains the meaning out of even the richest experiences."[1]

If you find you can't stuff anything more into your day, if a whirl of activity has depleted your energy, pull up a chair, sit down, take off your shoes, and give me a minute of your time.

You aren't the only woman to feel overwhelmed. You belong to a stressed-out sisterhood who have too much to do and too little time to do it. Leading our parade is none other than Martha. She was a capable woman who owned a home in Bethany that was frequented by Jesus. In fact, some scholars believe Martha's house may have been where "church" was held. It wouldn't surprise me since Martha was known for her ability to get things done. If you wanted good food, Martha could cook. If you wanted fancy decorations, Martha could design. If you wanted atmosphere, Martha could create. Everyone said her dinner parties were spectacular. And next on her docket was an event that had the entire town buzzing. Jesus and his friends were coming to dinner. This was going to be Martha's day to shine.

She had planned everything down to the most minute detail, because Martha never forgot a thing. Yet as the festivities were about to begin, the unexpected happened. Our hostess exploded.

If You Can't Stand the Heat, Get Out of the Kitchen

The appointed hour arrived. The food was hot. The guests were in place. But where was the help? Martha had organized this dinner party with two servers. She would take care of one side of the room, her sister, Mary, the other. Yet at the very moment when she needed Mary the most, the girl was nowhere to be found.

Martha looked in the bedroom, the back porch, the front porch, the dining room, and the kitchen. The only place she didn't look was in the living room. Mary would not be in there. That room had a sign over the door: "Men Only."

As Martha rushed by the room where the men were talking about important theological and social issues of the day, she could not believe what she saw. Like sand in her eyes, it was irritating. Sitting on the floor, gazing up intently at Jesus was her kid sister—little Miss Lazy.

"What are you doing in here?" Martha roared at her sister. "Why aren't you out in the kitchen helping me? Do I always have to do everything myself? Can't I ever get any help?"

Martha did not want to create a scene, but this time Mary had gone too far. Martha had always taken up the slack for her sister. Today was no different; however, it was the straw that broke Martha's back.

So she decided to use a new weapon. She would embarrass Mary in front of the guest of honor. Martha was certain Jesus had noticed how busy she was. She would enlist his help in getting Mary back into the kitchen where she belonged.

Looking at Jesus, Martha let loose a tirade: "Hey, doesn't it bother you that my sister has left me to do everything all by myself?"

The sudden flare-up took everyone off guard. Martha was so put together, so calm, so composed; this behavior was uncharacteristic.

But Jesus recognized that Martha's outburst came from a volcano of frustration that had finally erupted. Years of endless commotion and incessant activity had taken their toll, and Martha couldn't take anymore.

"Help me," she screamed.

The Man Who Invites You to Rest

Jesus looked at the stressed-out woman standing in front of him, dish towel in one hand, serving plate in the other.

"Martha, you are bothered about too much. You didn't have to go to all this trouble. You could have chosen to do one thing—the most important thing."

About this time in the conversation, I would have interrupted Jesus and said, "Stop right there. I've worked my fingers to the bone—and I did it all for you. Don't tell me my labor was for nothing. How ungrateful can you be?"

But I wasn't there. And before Martha could get another word out of her mouth, Jesus continued.

"Martha, take a look at your sister. I know she isn't in the kitchen helping you. But like you, she had to make a choice. And she chose better than you did. She chose to stop what she was doing and spend time with me."

A strange response to a woman who had just spent her day cooking and cleaning—not a good way to score points with a workaholic. A little appreciation for all the effort Martha had expended would have seemed more appropriate. But Jesus responded the way he did because he wanted Martha to recognize that her frustration was directly related to the choices she had made.

She chose to be busy. She chose to fill her day with activity. She chose to complicate her life. She would not slow down. She would not set boundaries. She would not say no. These were her choices. And now, Jesus was asking her to think about the choices that have caused her so much trouble. Jesus could not drag Martha out of the kitchen. He could not force her to sit down. He could not make her rest. However, he could invite her to rest. Choosing to rest with Jesus was her choice alone.

When confronted with so much to do, Martha thought all she needed was more help in the kitchen. Jesus's focus was on getting Martha out of the kitchen. He knew what Martha needed was permission to rest, and so he told her and every other workaholic woman that rest is all right. But in order to accept Jesus's gift, Martha had to stop doing what she thought was important. She had to focus on one thing at a time. And on this day, with Jesus in the house, resting at his feet was not only the best choice—it was the only choice.

Our Need—His Response

If you are completely overwhelmed, with the gas pedal to the floor, flying through each day at a breakneck pace, then put on the brakes. You need to take Jesus's advice to a woman suffering from the "Hurried Woman Syndrome." The crazy notion being tossed around that you can have it all and all at once is like a piece of Swiss cheese—there are holes in it. Jesus underlined this point when he told Martha, "You need to choose the most important thing and put it first!"

Jesus asked Martha and all the other members of her busybody gene pool to turn in their running shoes for a pair of comfortable slippers. He invites us to take time to rest at his feet each day. In fact, he has a spot marked out for you and one for me. And once we find our place in his presence, he will turn to us and say, "Are you tired? Worn out? Burned out? Come to me. Get away with me and you'll recover your life. I'll show you how to take a real rest. Walk with me and work with me—watch how I do it . . . I won't lay anything heavy or ill-fitting on you. Keep company with me and you'll learn to live freely and lightly" (Matt. 11:28–30 Message).

> Ask where the good way is, and walk in it, and you will find rest for your souls.
>
> Jeremiah 6:16 NIV

> The LORD your God is with you . . . he will quiet you with his love.
>
> Zephaniah 3:17 NIV

199

Sitting at your feet, you'd think I'd learn, yet each day seems to teem with failure, discouragement and letting everyone down, especially you. But you know what I appreciate? That with you all things are possible. That I can trust you even if I am fickle. And that though my promises falter, you, The Covenant Keeper, will always keep your word.[2]

Martha Borth

A Time for Reflection

The Stressed Woman: Martha of Bethany
Background Texts: Luke 10:38–41; John 11:1–39; 12:2

Exploration

My thoughts on feeling stressed . . .

1. What activities leave me feeling stressed each day?

2. If I had to choose to eliminate certain stressful activities, what would they be?

3. What are the three most important things I want to do in my life?
   A.
   B.
   C.

4. What activities do I identify as "essential" in my life?

> Be still before the LORD and wait patiently for him.
> Psalm 37:7 NIV

Inspiration

> They made me the keeper of the vineyards; but mine own vineyard have I not kept.
>
> Song of Solomon 1:6 AMP

I've always been intrigued by these words of Solomon. Evidently, even this capable king found he could take care of others better than himself—a common problem for super-women of the world who are experts at taking care of everyone else but letting things slide when it comes to their own lives.

Finding myself trying to perform a juggling act and dropping balls in the process, I perked up when my friend Adrianne invited me to attend a class on something she called "centering prayer."

When she mentioned she had been involved in this type of prayer for several years, she added, "I get up every day at 4:00 a.m. to pray." Right there she nearly lost me. At 4:00 a.m. I couldn't roll out of bed if I tried, but thankfully I think Adrianne knew me well enough and she continued by saying, "Now, Dorothy, not everyone chooses to pray at this time of day." I breathed a sigh of relief. With that assurance I joined Adrianne for the class on a type of praying I knew nothing about.

The instructor was Rusty Swavely, a lady whose poise and dignity drew me immediately into the circle of her presence. Over the next few weeks, as I attended a weekly prayer session, it became evident that Rusty was no being from an-

Note well the words of Jesus . . . It is not, "Go, labor on," as perhaps you imagine, [but] . . . "Come to Me and rest." Never, never did Christ send a heavy-laden one to work; never, never did He send . . . a weary one, a sick or sorrowing one away on any service. For such the Bible only says, "Come, come, come."

J. H. Taylor

201

other world untouched by the challenges that plague busy women on planet Earth. Instead, she was just like the rest of us, trying to balance work, family, and church responsibilities with many other unexpected events that, like a tidal wave, hit us in the spot that knocks us off our feet.

When Rusty began to explain the dynamic process of developing a relationship that invites the presence of God into our lives through times of silent sacredness, I have to admit, I thought this would be an impossible task for a girl like me who was used to perpetual motion.

During our class, each member selected a sacred word. I chose a phrase from the Psalms—"You are my strength"— as my focus for spiritual invitation for a period of twenty minutes. Then, in quietness, sitting in a comfortable chair, I began to filter out all the "clutter" that overwhelms my mind most of the time, and I kept coming back to the thought, "You are my strength."

To be quite honest, I thought the twenty minutes of silence would seem like an eternity. For me to be quiet and sit still seemed like an impossible request. But to my surprise, the time flew by.

Over the last few months, spending twenty minutes each day in quiet solitude, in the calm, restful presence of Jesus, has given a balance to my life that I desperately needed. And it has helped me understand why this type of prayer is called "centering prayer." It has helped me focus on what should be the center of my life—the spiritual core—that part of myself that when balanced makes everything else fall into place. This is why Jesus's instruction to Martha was, "If you will choose the most important thing in your life—the spiritual—and make it first, your entire life will stabilize—become steady." He knew that silent rest in a busy world was the key that unlocked the door to his presence. His open invitation awaits all of us busybodies: "Come with me by yourself to a quiet place and get some rest" (Mark 6:31 NIV).

1. How do I incorporate rest throughout my day? If resting is not part of my daily life, why and what can I do to change that?

2. What lessons on rest have I learned from Mary and Martha?

3. How can I accept Jesus's offer of rest?

> Silent in God's presence, you can relax yourself completely. The restfulness of being alone at last, facing reality, may even make you laugh aloud for joy as you open your mind in perfect confidence and summon the whole bustling medley of burdensome thoughts before Him. Let them come, waiting quietly for each, without a shadow of dread. See how they show up in the deep calm of God's presence.
>
> Muriel Lester, American theologian

Affirmation

Set your heart on God. . . . You'll forget your troubles; they'll be like old, faded photographs. Your world will be washed in sunshine . . . full of hope, you'll relax, confident again; you'll look around, sit back, and take it easy.

Job 11:16–18 Message

Misunderstood *(mis-un-der-stŏŏd)* v.

1. To misconstrue.

2. To misinterpret.

15

The Misunderstood Woman

> Six days before Passover, Jesus entered Bethany where La-
> zarus, so recently raised from the dead, was living. Lazarus
> and his sisters invited Jesus to dinner at their home. . . . Mary
> came in with a jar of very expensive aromatic oils, anointed
> and massaged Jesus' feet, and then wiped them with her hair.
> The fragrance of the oils filled the house.
>
> John 12:1–3 Message

During my senior year in high school, family and friends
began to ask a predictable question: "What are you planning to do with the rest of your life?" My answer: "I have
no idea!"

There wasn't any occupation that screamed out, "Dorothy,
this is for you!" In an attempt to help me focus on a produc-
tive career choice, my parents recommended I take one of
those aptitude tests that is supposed to tell you where your
interests lie. Well, so much for my answer. The two areas

205

where I scored highest pointed me in very different directions. The test results claimed I should either become a scientist or a florist. I preferred the florist direction—the adults in my life preferred science. So my dad and mother proposed what they called a compromise.

"Why don't you take nursing," my dad suggested. "Being a nurse will provide you with skills to acquire a good job while you're trying to figure out what you want to do." (Never say my parents weren't logical and practical.)

Just two short weeks after high school graduation, off to nursing school I went. My parents' assessment that becoming a Registered Nurse would help me get a good job was right on target. After taking and passing my California State Boards, I had four job offers. Finding a job was easy. Getting a job I liked was a lot harder.

It didn't take me long to realize new graduates often had little choice as to the hours they worked. One of my first regular positions at the local hospital was at night from 11:00 p.m. to 7:00 a.m. After a few months my body informed me that 4:00 a.m. was a time to sleep not work. So I applied for a new position on what, at that time, was called the "swing" shift, 3:00 p.m. to 11:00 p.m. For a young, single girl, this was a dream job. Most of the people throughout the hospital on our shift were young, and we became like a family. After we got off work we would go out for food and fun. It was a great life, enjoying the company of co-workers who were my best friends.

> We can sometimes love what we do not understand, but it is impossible completely to understand what we do not love.
>
> Anna Jameson,
> *A Commonplace Book*

One afternoon when I came on duty, ten out of twenty-four beds on our floor were empty. This meant one of two things. Either the workload would be light and some of us would be transferred to other areas, or our shift would be "hell" and we would get ten new patients.

The latter came true. There were several car accident victims who were taken from the emergency room directly to intensive care. Since our unit was right around the corner from intensive care, we received their overflow—patients who were well enough to transfer to our private rooms.

> To understand is to forgive, even oneself.
>
> Alexander Chase,
> *Perspectives*

As one new admission after another filled the beds, I realized three staff would never be enough to handle the load, so I called the supervisor and asked for some help. A few minutes later, the floor clerk informed me we were being sent Norma. She was the last person we wanted. First of all, she had a reputation for being a grump. And second, she was old enough to be our grandmother. I groaned. The clerk scowled. But when you're desperate—and we were—any warm body will do.

When Norma came to the desk to get her patient assignments, I could tell by the look on her face that she wasn't happy to be "floated" to our floor either. She kept referring to us as a "bunch of kids." I quickly went over the needs of each patient and told her I'd check back with her in a few minutes.

After passing out the evening medications, I stopped in the room where Norma was changing the bed of a patient who was very ill and had just thrown up. With a gentleness that I didn't know she possessed, Norma cleaned the elderly lady. She helped her to a chair and began to remake her bed—all the time talking in a kind, reassuring voice.

I was surprised by Norma's demeanor, to say the least. So I stopped and offered to help her finish changing the bed linens. "You don't have to help me," she said curtly. I ignored her remark and began to assist her in making the bed.

When we finished, I looked at Norma as I said, "On this floor we work as a team. We help each other."

"Really," she said, and the conversation ended.

By 11:00 p.m. when we were ready to go home, some of my co-workers mentioned that Norma had been a big help. They, too, had noticed how kind she was to her patients. We actually appreciated her help, and we told her so. Over the next few weeks, Norma ended up being transferred to our floor rather frequently. And one day, the supervisor came by with a request: "Norma has asked for a permanent transfer to this floor."

"I'm not surprised," I responded. "We want her to work here."

Now it was the supervisor who had a look of shock on her face. "May I ask you why you would want her? Everybody else complains about Norma, calling her the worst names. And you're telling me you actually want her here, permanently?"

"That's right," I said, "We like her."

The supervisor kept shaking her head. And so I began to tell her a little about Norma. After getting acquainted with her, we found out Norma was a widow left with a small pension that was totally inadequate. She had no children and no living relatives anywhere close. On holidays, birthdays, and sick days—Norma was alone. Life was a bitter pill, and swallowing that pill had left her with an upset stomach, a grouchy face, and a salty tongue. Norma decided she could give as good as she got!

What's more, we found out Norma wasn't the only person with a reputation. Norma told us that our little "clique" had been the topic of the hospital rumor mill too. We weren't the only ones coming to the table with preconceived notions. Norma had a few of her own. She had heard that our team was "a bunch of young, irresponsible party girls."

After a few nights of working together, not only did our

> The growth of understanding follows an ascending spiral rather than a straight line.
>
> Joanne Field,
> *A Life of One's Own*

attitude about Norma completely change, her opinion of us did too. With time and knowledge our understanding of each other was drastically altered. Rather than believing what we heard about Norma, we actually got to know her, and our personal contact provided us with information that enlightened us. The understanding that developed between us was the necessary ingredient to help us function as a well-oiled machine. And with Norma's help, that's what we became. Not only did patients ask to be transferred to our floor, physicians began to request that their patients be admitted to our area. What's more, they requested that Norma be assigned to their patients who were extremely ill.

Misunderstand. Misconstrue. Misinterpret.

Through the years, I have been reminded about Norma, especially when I've made one of those "jump-to-conclusion" assessments of another person only to find out later my snap judgment was incorrect. Have you had a similar experience? Did you ever form an opinion about someone based on their behavior or something you were told about that person, only to realize later your assumptions were completely off base?

Unfortunately, our multimedia, computer-driven, electronic world peppers us with so much data, and at such a frenzied pace, we are left little time to verify if the "facts" we receive have any connection to the truth. What's worse, our time-challenged lives often hamper our ability to get to know the people around us, and so it becomes easy to misinterpret their behavior or misconstrue their words. The consequence: misunderstandings fulminate. Incorrect information, interpreted falsely, affects our viewpoint and not only blocks the development of healthy relationships, but sometimes destroys them.

Whether it is some tabloid headline that catches my eye at the checkout counter in the grocery store or a phone call

209

that delivers titillating tongue talk about another person, innuendo and hearsay only serve to drive a stake through the heart of mutual understanding. And if ever there were a need for human hearts to be brought together through the gift of understanding, it is today.

How do we go about effectively incorporating this gift into our modern lifestyle? I decided that in order to get a better grasp of what it really means to *understand*, I would take a look at the original Hebrew and Greek meanings of this word that is used so frequently in both the Old and New Testaments. In fact, the wisest man who ever lived, Solomon, referred in the book of Proverbs to the word *understanding* over fifty times. Here are just a few of the meanings I found. In Hebrew the word *understand* is used to mean "intelligent consideration" (see Jer. 5:15). The psalmist, David, frequently used the word *understand* to reflect discernment, as in this text: "Make me to understand [discern] the way of your precepts" (Ps. 119:27 NRSV).

In the New Testament, the word *understanding*, in the Greek dictionary, has several meanings. Jesus used it to describe wisdom (see Matt. 13:13–15). Paul, in his letter to the Ephesians, used the word *understand* to encourage his readers to exercise their minds (see Eph. 3:4).

But of all the historical translations of this well-used word, the most interesting is the Hebrew, which is *yada*, meaning "to know by seeing, observing, caring, and recognizing." I find it interesting that our pop culture, encouraged by a television sitcom, has incorporated this language into current conversation with the phrase "yada, yada, yada," which we use as communication shorthand to let someone know they can figure out the rest of what we don't want to say. How ironic that rather than using this word to convey deeper understanding, as it truly means, we use it to abbreviate the information we give another person, thus causing the potential for more misunderstandings.

You and I could blame our rush-about world for the loss of understanding we have for one another, but to do so would be to ignore the obvious. It isn't just people in the twenty-first century who have lost their ability to understand one another. We aren't the only generation to misconstrue information and behavior. Human history is littered with the consequences of misunderstandings that went from a disagreement among friends to wars between nations. Even throughout Scripture, from Genesis to Revelation, misunderstandings dot the pages. When Jesus was on earth, he found the lack of understanding regarding his ministry and mission was to be a significant reason many individuals rejected him. The desire many people had for Jesus to become a human liberator, the champion who would unlock the chains of Roman oppression, obliterated his message of a heavenly kingdom rather than an earthly one.

A Misunderstood Maverick

Because Jesus had a personal familiarity with being misunderstood, it is not surprising that other individuals who faced the same problem were drawn to him. It was his sensitivity for those who were judged harshly for strange behavior, or for the place of their birth, or for the things they said, that served to highlight his open-hearted response to misunderstood misfits.

No wonder his spirit of kindness was so effective in drawing one woman out of a pit of misunderstanding. For if ever there were a person whom family, friends, and neighbors couldn't understand, it was Mary of Bethany. Someone was always "getting her wrong." Part of the problem may well have been Mary's behavior, which seemed to defy the rules. When you don't do things like everyone else, it is easy for people to misunderstand you. Maybe this is why, from the first time we meet Mary at her home to the last time we see her, causing a commotion at a community party, there is no doubt that she isn't a run-of-the-mill girl. The result: she is constantly being chastised for her unusual, some might

211

say "outlandish," antics. So if, like Mary, you have ever felt that no one understands you, then let's take a trip to a town called Bethany, a town whose name meant "house of dates and figs," a village located on the road to Jericho near the Mount of Olives.

Bethany was a rest stop Jesus called "home." It was the house where Martha, Lazarus, and their younger sister, Mary, lived, and there was always a welcome mat out to Jesus. What's more, Martha made certain there was food on the table. But on this day, if you were to look closely at the scene, you'll see that the men are in the living room discussing religion while the women are in the kitchen cooking. Sounds about right. Isn't that the way things are supposed to be? But I invite you to look again. There's one misplaced woman in the "men's quarters," sitting at the feet of Jesus, taking in every word that falls from his lips. And Jesus doesn't seem to mind. He isn't one bit concerned that a woman wants to spend time with him, rather than make stew or bake bread or do the dishes.

It was obvious Mary was a nonconformist, a woman flaunting the rules, a misunderstood maverick with a mission.

The Man Who Understands You (Better Than You Understand Yourself)

The story of the Good Samaritan is one of the most famous parables Jesus ever told. Interestingly, Jesus relates this story as he is making his way from Jerusalem to Bethany—a town that is a pit stop on the way to Jericho. This road was frequented by Jesus, for many times he had traversed the narrow, rocky terrain on his way to visit Mary, Martha, and Lazarus. As he spoke to his fellow travelers about the gracious kindness shown by the Samaritan to a stranger, he couldn't help but think about the times he had been welcomed with open arms and unselfish hospitality into the house of his friends.

On this particular day, Jesus wanted to avail himself of the warmth of a "genial hearth." It was in this accepting environment, surrounded by his disciples and one woman, where Jesus gave his first lesson on understanding individuals who aren't doing what we think they should be doing.

I call this event "Misunderstanding Number 1," and it is a spiritual misunderstanding, caused by the entrenched customs in a culture that dictated to women the place they could occupy in religious society. Ring any bells? And although this incident took place over two thousand years ago, Jesus's lesson is applicable today.

At the time of Jesus's ministry, women were considered second-class citizens. Josephus, the noted Jewish historian, wrote that a woman "is in every respect less worth than a man"![1] Women were generally grouped with children and even slaves. Women were often viewed as incapable of comprehending religious matters. As noted by author Michael Griffiths in *The Example of Jesus*: "It is not clear that all rabbis taught what Rabbi Eliezer ben Azariah teaches in the Talmud and Mishnah—he may have been an extremist in his views, but he is reported as saying: 'It is better that the words of the law should be burned than that they should be given to a woman.' And again, 'If a man gives his daughter a knowledge of the law, it is as though he taught her lechery.' "[2]

To more clearly delineate the spiritual role of women at this time, Joachim Jeremias wrote: "In the temple a woman was allowed access only as far as the Court of the Women. Her religious obligations were on the same level as that of a slave; for example, she did not have to pray the Shema morning and evening, because like a slave she was not mistress of her own time."[3]

With this historical setting, it is easy to understand why Martha became so annoyed when her sister chose to join the men and participate in Jesus's "discussion group." Women were supposed to cook the food, serve the food, and clean up after the food was eaten. Mary's behavior challenged routine practice. It flew in the face of customary behavior. Her conduct was unorthodox. And so Martha enlisted the help of Jesus to get the renegade back into the kitchen where she belonged.

However, Jesus informed everybody in the home that Mary's behavior was perfectly all right with him. In fact, he honored her by saying she had chosen well, and if no one else could understand her spiritual choice, he could (see Luke 10:41).

Jesus made it crystal clear that spending time with him was more important than following tradition. And I am going to go out on a limb here, but a limb nourished by the words of Jesus, and say to ladies everywhere that answering the call of Jesus, in any capacity where he has need of your talents, takes priority over any ritual, any custom, any man-made rule, no matter how misunderstood your behavior may be. Mary wasn't a woman fighting for her rights; she was fighting for her life—her spiritual life. This was a woman who wanted to walk with Jesus, and for Mary, that meant taking a path untraveled by others. I'm so thankful Jesus understood and honored Mary's choice.

The next time we see Mary, tragedy had struck her family. Her brother, Lazarus, had been taken ill. Even though a message was sent to Jesus to come quickly, he chose to wait two days to arrive, and by the time he got to Bethany, Lazarus was dead. When Martha heard Jesus was nearing their home, in her typical in-your-face manner she ran out of the house, met Jesus on the road, and chastised him by saying: "Lord, if thou hadst been here, my brother had not died" (John 11:21 KJV). And while this was happening where was Mary? John tells us: "Mary sat still in the house" (John 11:20 KJV). And this brings us to "Misunderstanding Number 2." What I consider an emotional misunderstanding.

With mourners howling around the house and Martha giving Jesus a lecture about tardiness, Mary chose to "sit still" in the house. I can just imagine people looking at her and wondering why she was acting in such an unusual manner. This was weeping and wailing time, and here was Mary, being quiet. At this point in time we are told Martha came back to the house and "secretly" said to Mary, "The Master is come, and he calleth for thee" (John 11:28 KJV).

Immediately, Mary left the house and ran to Jesus, the one person she knew who would understand her, even if her expression of pain wasn't like everybody else's. And here's the part of this event I just love. Although I had read this story before, I missed a critical detail until now. John says that "when Jesus therefore saw [Mary] weeping . . . he groaned in the spirit, and was troubled, and asked 'Where have ye laid him?' . . . Jesus wept" (John 11:33–35 KJV). The Greek translation sheds even more light on this moment by saying Jesus "sobbed aloud."

The understanding master of Mary's life looked into her eyes and felt the pain his child was suffering and he broke down and wept with her. Why? Because Mary's pain was his pain. Her grief was his grief. He wept because he understood how she felt. Doesn't Jesus's response give you comfort? For when the knife of pain penetrates your heart, he's hurting too. And those tears that are rolling down your cheeks are streaming down his face too.

Several days later, Mary appears again, but this time it isn't a time of quiet in her home or mourning at her brother's grave. It's celebration time, a "thank-you Jesus" event held six days before Passover in Bethany. At the head of the table sat Jesus and Lazarus—the raised-from-the-dead star attraction. As usual, Martha is serving the supper. And as usual, Mary isn't anywhere to be seen.

Not long after the festivities began, a pungent odor wafted throughout the dining room, and an aroma turned heads. And then Mary appeared! She was at it again, loosening her long, flowing hair, and wiping Jesus's feet with the contents of an expensive and rare bottle of "nard" or perfume. The girl poured the bottle out on Jesus's feet and on the floor. What a waste! Here comes "Misunderstanding Number 3," and it's a doozy! This was a behavioral misunderstanding that set the entire room abuzz with *oohs* and *aahs*. One of the first people to jump on the "you shouldn't act like this" bandwagon was Judas Iscariot, who was quick to point out that "the perfume could be sold for three hundred denari (a year's wages for an ordinary workman) and that the money could have been given to the poor (see John 12:5 AMP). At this point in time, I think King David's words are appropriate: "Be not like . . . the mule, which lack[s] understanding" (Ps. 32:9 AMP). Like a braying donkey, Judas—the "treasurer"—decided to make a spectacle of Mary's wasteful use of money. But what do you think the other people in the room would have thought had they acquired the knowledge—the discernment—to understand that in just a matter of days, Judas would sell his friend, Jesus, for half the amount of Mary's extravagant gift?

As the embarrassed Mary hurried to leave the room, Jesus interrupted the chaos with these words: "Let her alone. . . . You always have the poor with you, but you do not always have Me" (John 12:7–8 AMP).

Mary may have been misunderstood because she didn't behave like everybody else; however, her time with Jesus opened her eyes to the three ingredients essential to acquiring heavenly understanding. First, Mary had to stop what she was doing. She even had to put aside what others thought she should do. She had to put Jesus first. Second, she had to listen to him. In the words of Jesus, "[She] who has ears to hear, let [her] be listening, and consider and perceive and comprehend by hearing" (Matt. 11:15 AMP). Spending time listening to Jesus gave Mary knowledge—and it was this knowledge that proved to be the foundation that helped her understand not only Jesus's ministry to others but his work in her life as well.

How do I know this? Mary's actions tell the story. For of all the followers of Jesus, Mary of Bethany was the only one who Jesus commended for preparing him for his burial (see John 12:7 AMP). She was the only person who said thank you to Jesus before he died. Her time with Jesus had given her the understanding to know what she could do for him.

Our Need—His Response

Before I got to know Mary, I wondered what need she had that Jesus could respond to. She wasn't sick. She wasn't destitute. She wasn't alone. She had a family. She had friends. She had a home. She was a lot like many people I know. From the outside looking in, Mary's life seemed "charmed." But as we lift the curtain on each act in Mary's life, we find a woman who, like so many of us, was seeking to understand who she was and where she fit in. What I discovered as I studied Mary's life was that sometimes her search led her into unexplored territory. This may have happened to you too. You may have found there have been times when in your search for understanding, you have wandered into a wilderness, not knowing where you are or what you should do.

If like Mary, you are searching for that one person who understands you better than you understand yourself, I have a news alert, your search is over!

Like Mary at the feet of Jesus, you will find the understanding you thought was impossible. You'll find a friend who understands you spiritually. Who understands you emotionally. And what's more, he understands your behavior, even when no one else does.

When I was recovering from the car accident that took away my ability to walk for many months, on one particularly painful day I was in the hospital gym on a large, flat, padded table, trying as best I could to lift my legs. The exercise was difficult, and the pain excruciating. As I repeatedly tried to obey the commands of the physical therapist, I began to cry, not out loud, but just silent tears running down my face. My sister was standing by the mat, holding my hand. As I looked at her, I saw tears rolling down her cheeks too. We didn't have to say a word. It was a moment of understanding when two hearts were beating as one. It's rare in our lives to have times when we grasp the content of another's heart. But with Jesus, we know he always understands our heart, because he is walking our path

217

with us. In the words of my favorite poet, Emily Dickinson, "Unto a broken heart, no other one may go, without the high prerogative, itself hath suffered too."

How grateful I am that the understanding Mary longed for, the understanding you and I yearn for, is always found in the presence of Jesus. As the apostle Paul found out, "Now that we know what we have—Jesus, this great High Priest with ready access to God—let's not let it slip through our fingers. We don't have a [friend] who is out of touch with our reality. He's been through weakness and testing, experienced it all . . . So let's walk right up to him and get what he is so ready to give. . . . Accept the help" (Heb. 4:14–16 Message).

> And we . . . know that the Son of God has [actually] come to this world and has given us understanding and insight progressively to perceive [recognize] . . . more clearly Him Who is true.
>
> 1 John 5:20 AMP

A Time for Reflection

The Misunderstood Woman: Mary of Bethany
Background Texts: Mark 14:3–9; Luke 10:39–42; John 11:1–20, 28–45; 12:1–9

Exploration

My thoughts on being misunderstood . . .

1. If I could identify one area of my life where I feel spiritually misunderstood, what would it be?

2. If I could identify one area in my life where I feel emotionally misunderstood, what would it be?

3. If I could identify one area in my life where I feel as though my behavior has been misunderstood, what would it be?

4. How do I respond when those around me misunderstand my behavior?

5. Is there a person in my life whom I have difficulty understanding?
   How and in what ways did I try to understand this person and his/her behavior?

> Though it cost all you have, get understanding. Esteem her, and she will exalt you: embrace her, and she will honor you. She will set a garland of grace on your head and present you with a crown of splendor.
>
> Proverbs 4:7–9 NIV

Inspiration

> Real charity [love] and a real ability never to condemn—the one real virtue—is so often the result of a waking experience that gives a glimpse of what lies beneath things.
>
> Ivy Compton-Burnett (1913)

It was a cold day by Arizona standards. A chilly wind blew as family and friends gathered at the cemetery to lay to rest a mother and friend—Laura Buick. Her death was not unexpected, for she was ninety-eight years old.

The pastor began to quietly read words written by Laura's daughter—a tribute to a loving mother. As the story of Laura's life unfolded, I was shocked by what I heard.

When Laura was just three years old, her father beat her pregnant mother to death. On the evening of her mother's funeral, relatives took Laura to the local orphanage and left her.

219

When Laura turned six, a family member needed someone to work at her boarding house. She came to the orphanage and got Laura, not because she loved her, but because her labor came at no cost.

Laura never finished elementary school. Her holey shoes and raggedy clothes made walking to school in the snowy Chicago winters impossible.

It would be twenty-two years before anyone ever told Laura she was loved.

As I looked around at the faces of the people standing at the graveside, I saw tears rolling down many cheeks, and I wondered if others were thinking the same thing I was: *Would I have been a better friend to Laura if I had known more about her? Would I have been kinder and more loving if I had taken time to really get to know her and to understand the circumstances that had shaped her life?*

Someone observed that it is best to treat the people we meet as if their hearts are breaking—because they probably are. Knowing what lies beneath would give us the discernment to understand.

> Love of our neighbor in all its fullness simply means being able to say to [her], "What are you going through?"
>
> Simone Weil, *Waiting for God*

1. How would I have reacted if I were Martha and saw Mary sitting with Jesus while I was working?

2. How would I have reacted to Mary's response when Lazarus died?

3. How would I have reacted to Mary's behavior when she anointed Jesus at the feast?

4. What would I have thought about the cost of her gift?

5. If I had been in the room that day and had no knowledge of Judas's past and future behavior, how would I have felt about his outburst?

6. Just as Jesus spent time getting to know Mary, who is there in my life that with time and knowledge I might understand better?

> And we know that the Son of God came so we could recognize and understand the truth of God.
>
> 1 John 5:20 Message

> All, everything I understand, I understand because I love.
>
> Leo Tolstoy, *War and Peace*

Affirmation

> The way you tell me to live is always right; help me understand it so I can live to the fullest.
>
> Psalms 119:144 Message

Ambitious *(ăm-bish'as)* adj.

1. *Greatly desirous.*

2. *Aggressive.*

3. *Hard-driving.*

16

The Ambitious Woman

At this point the mother of the sons of Zebedee arrived with her sons and knelt in front of Jesus to ask him a favor. 'What is it you want?' he asked her. "Please say that these two sons of mine may sit one on each side of you when you are king!" she said. "You don't know what it is you are asking," replied Jesus.

Matthew 20:20–22 Phillips

Bethanie, Aimee, and Effie—looking through photograph albums that detailed the events of their lives.

We laughed as we saw pictures of camping trips, vacations, birthday celebrations, and graduations—memories recorded by photos, snapshots of our past that left a record of time spent together.

One event stood out, not because of the occasion or who was in the photograph. This picture left a record of who was not there. I was not in the photo. The event was Aimee's graduation. I could not go. Well, let me rephrase it; I *did* not go.

> Men in high places are driven by insatiable ambition to clutch at still greater prizes. And nowhere is there any final satisfaction, because nothing there can be defined as absolutely the best or the highest.
>
> Bernard of Clairvaux,
> *On Loving God*

Our company was busy. A group of potential new clients was having a convention. They called and asked me to hold a workshop, an all-day affair. I was thrilled. This would provide an excellent opportunity to sell new business, and I was certain it could add substantially to our client base.

It was a good business decision. And since the request for me to speak came several months before the conference, I hastily added the date to my schedule, giving no thought to personal conflicts.

I had been given the date of Aimee's graduation months before, but I failed to write it in my appointment book. So the day she called to remind me, I did not know what to say. The date conflicted with my business meeting.

Finally, I got up the courage to blurt out the words, "Honey, you know I would be there if I could, but I will be out of town at a very important conference. I am one of the speakers. I hope you understand."

She let me off the hook. "Oh, Effie, you do so much for me already, it doesn't matter. Don't worry about it."

A few weeks later I headed to California for my presentation. As I pulled into the parking lot at the conference center, I noticed things seemed very quiet. I walked over to the parking booth and asked the attendant where the workshops were being held. He instructed me to drive to the top of the hill. As I walked away he called out, "By the way, a lot of the people left this morning. There was an emergency they had to take care of, and they needed to get back to their offices."

The bottom line—six people showed up for my "big" workshop. The registration had been for over fifty. What I thought would be a business bonanza was a business bust.

As we reviewed the photographs, Aimee pointed to the picture and said, "Oh, that's my graduation. You couldn't come, Effie. Remember?"

How could I forget? The people invited to the conference do not remember me. They forgot long ago. In fact, they probably forgot before they left the parking lot—but not Aimee. She remembered I was not there.

Ambitious. Aggressive. Pushy.

I wish I could tell you that missing Aimee's graduation was the only time I have let the fires of ambition blow out of control, clouding my judgment to the point where I let someone down because my priorities were out of whack.

Regrettably, all too often I have found myself running head-long into the consequences of putting the wrong things first. Has this ever happened to you—upside-down and twisted priorities?

In a world that exalts the accomplishments of the ambitious, it is easy to get off track. And before we know it, we find ourselves going in the wrong direction. Even when we are rewarded with the so-called transient trappings of accomplishment, we can find earthly ambition to be a demanding taskmaster that is not satisfied by earthly achievement.

As I rush to grab each rung on the ladder of success, pushing my way through the crowd and hoping for a better position or bigger paycheck, I wonder, "Where will this race for a top spot get me?"

Not long ago I stumbled upon this golden nugget, an insight shared by C. S. Lewis as he analyzed our quest to find ultimate happiness: "We are halfhearted creatures, fooling about with drink and sex and ambition when infinite joy is offered us, like an ignorant child who wants to go on making mud pies in a slum because he cannot imagine what is meant by the offer of a holiday at sea." Am I going to be happy when I reach the top of the "heap" because that is all I can imagine? Or when I get to the top will I find that indeed it is just a "heap" after all?

When Success Isn't What You Think It Is

A few days ago, a close friend called and said, "I want to give you a quiz."

"Why?" I asked.

"Just go along with me on this," she urged, so I agreed, and here are the questions she asked me:

- Name the five wealthiest people in the world.
- Name the last five Heisman trophy winners.
- Name the last five winners of the Miss America pageant.
- Name five people who have won the Pulitzer Prize.
- Name the last five academy award winners for best actor and actress.

When she finished I told her she must be kidding. I did not have the foggiest idea who most of these people were.

"Well," she continued, "I have some more questions for you."

- List five teachers who made a difference in your life.
- Name three friends who helped you through a difficult time.
- Name five people you like spending time with.
- Name five people who taught you something worthwhile.
- Name five people who have inspired you.

I did not have any trouble coming up with names of people who had encouraged me or people who had given me the gift of their time and talents. These were the individuals who had made a major difference in my life. Yet all too often, when we think of the pinnacle of success, we focus on "stars" who are rich and beautiful, followed by the paparazzi and adored by their fans.

Frankly, I would have felt like a total failure pushing my way up the "success" ladder if I had not run into Salome. What a relief to meet another woman struggling with her priorities. And what a great teacher Salome is because she was one of those real go-getters. Some might call her pushy. I believe she was just an ambitious woman who wanted to make certain her family did well. And there's nothing wrong with wanting the best for those you love.

Go to the Top of the Heap

Salome was watching—an interested mother, a concerned parent. Her sons had taken up with a carpenter from Nazareth, a day laborer from nowhere, named Jesus. Salome began to wonder, *Is this guy good enough to associate with my boys?*

Her children were "somebodys" from "somewhere." Their dad, Zebedee, was a man of means, a successful businessman with a sizeable staff and his own boat for deep-water fishing. Her kids had status and money. And Salome didn't want them settling for less than the best. So she watched. Who was Jesus? Was he big enough for her family? If the crowds that followed him were any indication, Jesus did seem to be popular. But anyone who could turn plain water into wine or feed five thousand people with two loaves of bread and five fish was bound to be popular. So Salome kept watching. And as the crowds grew . . . her hopes soared.

This man might be the longed-for deliverer, the man who would release Judea from the domination of Roman tyranny. And if Jesus truly was the one people thought he might be, and if he established a new government, just think what it would

227

mean for her family, especially her boys, if they had the inside track to Jesus! Direct access to the king. A hotline to the palace. These were the thoughts that began to roll around in Salome's head. Her small ideas grew into grandiose plans. Walking a dusty road with Jesus turned into a highway to the throne. Yes, I think we can agree, Salome had ambitious plans.

But what's more, Salome was willing to put her money where her mouth was.

Author Ron Brownrigg notes, "Zebedee allowed and enabled his wife Salome to give financial help to Jesus and his disciples." I can't say Zebedee and Salome gave money to Jesus hoping he would return the favor by honoring their sons, but let's just say it would not have been the first time in history that parents have used their financial power to pave the way for a son or daughter. What we do know is that their gifts to support Jesus certainly were noticed by the other disciples.

Once Salome had the "money-thing" going for her, she had one thing left to do. She had to maneuver to get Jesus alone. She wanted to speak with him one-on-one. She would use all her charms of persuasion to ask him for a favor. How could he deny her—a mother—a request on behalf of her children?

Finally the right moment arrived, and like a viper, Salome struck. "When you become the King, please put one of my boys on your right side and the other on your left" (see Matt. 20:20–22). In other words, "When you become the Chairman of the Board, make one of my boys president, and the other CEO."

Salome didn't want her kids to have to start at the bottom and work their way up. She wanted the top spots for her boys. Successful children would be a feather in her cap, a highlight on the family résumé. Her friends would be jealous. Power, fame, and wealth all rolled up together—just think what it would mean!

With eager anticipation Salome waited, hoping Jesus would give her exactly what she had asked. But to her surprise and disappointment, he didn't.

The Man Who Carries a Map

Salome was not prepared for Jesus's response, for it was not what she had expected or wanted to hear.

"Salome, you don't know what you are asking for. You have no idea where your request is going to take you and your family" (see Matthew 20:20–24).

> Do not care overly much for wealth, or power, or fame, or one day you will meet someone who cares for none of these things, and you will realize how poor you have become.
>
> Rudyard Kipling

Like a glass of cold water being tossed in her face, Salome was given a "reality check." But Jesus did it for her own good. He knew something Salome did not—her priorities were not in the right place. He knew the road she was on would not take her where she really wanted to go. Jesus knew that deep in her heart what Salome really wanted for her children was a life filled with purpose. That's because Jesus knew Salome better than she knew herself. She had proven by her example that she, too, was a follower of Jesus. She walked with him. She believed his message. And his call to service had taken root in her heart.

Since Jesus knew Salome and her family would never find their way into his kingdom going down a road paved by pleasure and ease, instead of giving Salome what she initially asked for, Jesus gave her what she needed—a road map clearly marked with directions to his kingdom.

Then he invited Salome to come on a journey with him. But she had to revise her expectations of the trip. "Salome," Jesus told her "on the road to my Kingdom you'll meet a King—but look closely. The crown he wears will be made of thorns. He won't be sitting on a throne. You'll see him kneeling like a servant. And if your boys follow his path, it will lead them through the valley of exile and martyrdom."

You might think that honesty like this would scare Salome away, but it didn't. This mother, who wanted earthly greatness for her children, chose to lead by example and accept Jesus's offer of heavenly service. If we follow the path Salome chose for herself, we will find her in an upper room, serving dinner to Jesus and his disciples. We will be present as this astonished mother watches Jesus bend down like a common servant and wash twelve pairs of dirty feet. We will follow Salome as she stands at a cross on a hill, surrounded by jeering Roman soldiers and an unrepentant thief. And in the early morning hours we will walk with her to a tomb that contains an angelic message to a mother whose example served to mark the path Salome's boys chose to take. No wonder Salome's son John never complained when exiled to the island of Patmos. No wonder her son James never turned from the road that led to his martyrdom. This mother had shown her boys what really counted in life. She had taught them what real success was all about. She had led with her example.

Salome thought she had the road to success mapped out perfectly, but the sign saying "Fame Here" would not give her family the fulfillment they wanted. The road called "Power Trip" did not lead to purpose. The path labeled the "Good Life" did not lead to a final destination of "Eternal Life."

So Jesus gave Salome exactly what she needed when he handed her a well-marked map with directions to his kingdom. It was a map this mother followed—a map she gave to her sons. A map that took them in a heavenly direction.

Our Need—His Response

"Where are you going?"

"What will you receive when you arrive at your destination?"

Like hidden treasure, these questions lie buried in Jesus's response to Salome because they force each of us to reassess our priorities.

Am I headed in the right direction? And in the end, will I find a reward that satisfies me for more than a fleeting moment?

Salome was pointed in the wrong direction, pushing and pulling to get to the top. So the man with the map marked out

a new route for her and her family. Jesus still carries a map
and he offers it to you and me. He has plans all laid out with
our names on them. Don't you feel more confident when you
have the directions in your hand and an experienced guide by
your side? "For what will it profit a [woman], if she gains the
whole world and forfeits [herself]? Or what will a [woman]
give in exchange for [her] soul?" (Matt. 16:26).

> What kind of a deal is it to get everything you want but lose
> yourself? What could you ever trade your soul for?
>
> Matthew 16:26 Message

> Money, power, and success can do nothing in the face of
> death; they can do nothing in the face of fear or terror; they
> can do nothing to change you from nobody to somebody and
> give you title to eternity: they can't do that.
>
> Peter J. Gomes, minister, the Memorial Church,
> Harvard University

A Time for Reflection

The Ambitious Woman: Salome
Background Texts: Matthew 27:56–61; 28:1; Mark 15:40–47;
  6:1; Luke 24:10

Exploration

My thoughts on ambition . . .

1. How do I define the word *success*?

2. What are my five highest priorities? List in order.
   A.
   B.
   C.
   D.
   E.

3. What criteria did I use to choose my priorities?

> Aim at heaven and you get earth thrown in; aim at earth and you get neither.
>
> C. S. Lewis

Inspiration

> Start with GOD—the first step in learning is bowing down to GOD . . . pay close attention . . . never forget what you learned at your mother's knee.
>
> Proverbs 1:7–8 Message

I often wonder what Dorothy Irene Hardin thought when, in her late thirties and with a six-month-old baby who was the last of nine children, she realized she was so ill she was going to die.

What dreams would you and I have for a baby we would never be able to raise?

As that little boy grew up, no one ever told him much about his mother until one eventful day. A group of young teens in the small town where he lived went to visit Mrs. Gammage, a well-known woman whose husband was president of the local college. Mrs. Gammage asked each child to step forward and tell her their names. One by one the young people introduced themselves. And then Jimmy Hardin stepped forward. As soon as Mrs. Gammage heard his name she spoke up. "Jimmy," she asked, "was your mother named Dot Hardin?" "I think so," the young man responded.

And then Mrs. Gammage did something for this orphan boy that forever changed his life. She told him about the mother he never knew.

"Jimmy," she said, "you had the most wonderful mother. I never heard her say a bad word about anyone. She worked for me, and she was always humming or whistling a tune. She was such a Christian and the most cheerful person I ever met."

Jimmy Hardin was my father. He told me years later, "When I heard what a wonderful mother I had, I purposed in my heart to make her proud and to be the kind of son she would have wanted me to be."

I was named after Dot Hardin, a grandmother I never met but a woman whose example has been followed by her family. Wouldn't she be happy to know that the legacy of a short life well lived has followed her for generations?

The story of Salome is also a story of a mother who left a cherished legacy for her family when she chose to follow the servant King.

1. What lessons can I learn from Salome?

2. If Jesus asked me, "Where are you going, and do you know what you will get when you arrive at your destination?" what would my answer be?

3. How can I lead my family by my example?

4. If I found out I had one year to live, how would my priorities change?

> A tragic irony of life is that we so often achieve success or financial independence after the reason for which we sought it has passed.
>
> Ellen Glasgow

Affirmation

Anyone who intends to come with me has to let me lead. You're not in the driver's seat—I am. Don't run from suffering; embrace it. Follow me and I'll show you how. Self-help is no help at all. Self-sacrifice is the way, my way, to finding yourself, your true self.

Luke 9:23–24 Message

Worthless *(wûr th'l 'ls)* adj.

1. Devoid of worth, use, or value.

2. Lacking dignity or honor.

3. Lacking all worth and value.

17

The Worthless Woman

And he sat down opposite the treasury, and watched the multitude putting money into the treasury. Many rich people put in large sums. And a poor widow came, and put in two copper coins, which make a penny. And he called his disciples to him, and said to them, "Truly, I say to you, this poor widow has put in more than all those who are contributing to the treasury. For they all contributed out of their abundance; but she out of her poverty has put in everything she had, her whole living."

Mark 12:41–44 RSV

I was fifteen years old when I got my first after-school job. Finally, I had money I could call my own! I thought I was wealthy.

After lengthy wrangling with my parents, I convinced them to let me keep half of my paycheck each month. Adhering to my part of the bargain, I went to the bank with my mother and deposited half of the money in a savings account—then, with great fanfare, I took the rest home and put the cash in a bottle on my dresser.

For months I was able to keep from spending my personal loot. Instead, I chose to keep the bottle where I could gaze on my riches. The day came, however, when I could no longer resist. I had to buy something, and there was no question what it would be.

Shoes. At an early age, I was an unapologetic shoe addict.

Growing up in a "practical" family, I had two pairs of shoes—one for every day and one for special occasions. But I wanted more. I watched as my friends at school paraded around the hallways in a variety of colorful shoes, and I was envious. I wanted more than a sturdy pair of black leather buckle shoes. I was a woman of wealth. I could change my plight. Webb's Department Store was my answer.

I asked my mother to take me downtown, and once inside the store I headed straight for the sign that said "SHOES."

As I looked over the display my eyes fell on just the perfect pair: tan flats with suede on the top, leather on the sides, and thin matching strings that tied.

I asked the salesman to please see if they had a pair in my size. In a few minutes he returned with a box marked size 6.

Quickly I slipped into the shoes, letting the salesman tie perfect bows in the strings. I stood up and started strutting around on the shiny linoleum. To this day, I can still hear the clicking of those shoes on the floor.

Within minutes I grabbed my wallet, paid the clerk, and was out the door, all the time thinking about the next day when I would wear my new shoes to school and show off to my friends.

That day was the beginning of many trips to many shoe stores. As I grew older and my paychecks grew, I was able to feed my "shoe appetite" with the ultimate—designer shoes.

I felt I had arrived the day I was sitting in the Beverly Hills Neiman-Marcus on Wilshire Boulevard with a stack of

Let us not seek wealth, nor high social position. These are external things. Let us seek true nobility of soul.

John Chrysostom, *Homily*

236

> What we obtain too cheap we esteem too little; it is dearness only that gives everything its value.
>
> Thomas Paine

Manolo Blanick shoeboxes surrounding me. If this were the pinnacle, I had reached it. The days of two pairs of shoes and Webb's Department Store were in the past. I had moved up in the world. If only my friends could see me now.

Then it happened. In one fateful moment, my shoe world came crashing down.

The day was August 28, 1997. The time—6:00 p.m.

My husband, Jim, and I were hit head-on by a drunk driver who was going over 70 mph. The force of the impact was so great it took an hour for the "jaws of life" to pry us from the wreckage.

For days the physicians did not believe we would survive. Miraculously, we did.

However, because the front of our car was destroyed, our feet and legs sustained multiple, crushing fractures. The doctors told us we probably would never walk again. And it was certain, if we did walk, it would be slowly and with great pain.

After four months in the hospital we were discharged to two years of outpatient rehabilitation. As time passed, the therapists patiently taught us to walk, first with the assistance of walkers, then crutches, and finally canes.

But in order to walk we had to find the right shoes. And believe me, I had a pretty good idea my new shoes were not going to be gorgeous designer shoes.

Our doctors told us about a man named Ernesto. He had a reputation for making the impossible happen. He was a shoe designer, but his specialty was constructing individual shoes for people with injured feet.

With the assistance of my new "designer" shoes, which have lifts and pads and cutouts, I am able to walk. My new shoes are not pretty. They do not look anything like my gorgeous Manolo Blanicks. But when I put on my plain, padded, black leather shoes, I am able to walk again. My new shoes are the perfect shoes for my broken, twisted feet.

Months after the accident, when I was back home, I hobbled into my closet and looked at the rows of fancy shoes on the shelf. Beautiful, colorful shoes, but totally unusable. I could not walk when I put them on. All of a sudden the value of my shoes was no longer dependent on what they looked like on the outside, but on how my feet felt on the inside when I took each step. At one time, my shoes were fashion accessories, a statement of my self-worth, as pathetic as that may sound. But in one split second my sense of what was valuable was turned upside down.

Worthless. Useless. Good-for-Nothing.

How much do you think you are worth? If someone said they would pay a million dollars for you, would it be enough?

Please don't laugh. Nobody I know goes around town with a price tag stuck on her back. Yet, inside we all carry a sense of our own value, a value that may be determined by what others have said about us, or by the clothes we wear, or the degrees behind our names, or the size of our bank accounts, or even by the shoes on our feet. Unfortunately, the value we attach to ourselves often translates into the way we view others.

Just think for a minute. How does our society go about placing worth on individuals such as:

- A company president or the building janitor.
- A professional athlete or the local schoolteacher.
- A baby born in Somalia or a baby born in Beverly Hills.

How is it that we go about assessing value to ourselves and to others?

For women this becomes a very personal question with implications that touch on everything from age to looks to

238

> God does not love us because we are valuable. We are valuable because God loves us.
>
> Archbishop Fulton J. Sheen

clothes and more. To hear some people talk you would think that a few wrinkles and a little fat define a woman as a worthless old bag. Facing forty, a once glamorous model feels washed up. So we color our hair, get our tummies tucked and faces lifted, hoping to recapture the allure that makes us feel as though we are valuable and worth something.

Should my personal worth be established by my financial status or job title? By the clothes on my back or the shoes on my feet? Absolutely not. Yet in reality none of us can honestly say there have not been times in our lives when we compared our personal value to material status symbols.

Recently, I was reading *Selected Writings*, a book written by Robert Ellsberg about the 1930s Catholic activist Dorothy Day, who was a tireless advocate for the poor. Those who worked closely with Dorothy were often astonished at the way she treated people, regardless of their social position.

One particular event left a lasting impression on the volunteers who assisted Dorothy. The incident took place in New York City. A wealthy woman donated a beautiful diamond ring to benefit Dorothy's programs.

The staff wondered what Dorothy would do with the expensive ring. If she sold it she could buy a great deal of food—a month's supply of beans for the hungry. Or she could pay the rent on their office building for a year.

Instead, Dorothy chose to give the ring to a poor woman who came regularly for bowls of food. The workers protested. But Dorothy replied, "That poor woman has her dignity too." The poverty-stricken woman could sell the ring if she liked and spend the money for rent, a trip to the Bahamas, or she could even keep the ring to admire. It didn't matter to Dorothy. "Do you suppose God created diamonds only for the rich?" she reflected.

If you have ever wondered how valuable you really are, you need look no further than a treasury box at church where a group of people got into a discussion. The topic: money and personal value. This was the premise on which the conversation was based: if you are wealthy, you are valuable; if you are poor, you are worthless.

When Mites Equal Millions

Jesus was teaching in a porch at the temple. Surrounded by his disciples he began to give everyone a lesson on money. Maybe it was a topic that was weighing heavily on his mind because of a conversation he had with a young man who had earlier come to him asking which commandment was the most important. Jesus's reply noted that the commandments could be summarized in two statements: First, love God supremely, and second, love your neighbor as you would yourself. From this dialogue, Jesus began to set the stage for an event known as the offering of the widow's mite. After specifically warning religious leaders, in particular, not to "devour widow's homes and then cover their greedy behavior with long prayers" (see Mark 12:40), Jesus placed himself in a position where he could watch as crowds came with their gifts for the temple treasury.

This was a particularly busy day. It was the end of Passover week. Thousands of Jews had come to the city of Jerusalem during this holiest of feasts. For many, this was a time not only for the confession of sin but also for the remittance of offerings. And at the end of the week, just before sundown, a widow entered the courtyard.

Times had been tough for this woman. Mark wrote that she was "poverty stricken." From this descriptive phrase, we can only imagine what a meager pittance she had to live on. Many women at this time in history found their financial security directly related to the status of their husbands. Possibly her husband died young, leaving her without a "nest egg" for a rainy day. He may have had debts that others came to collect from his estate. Whatever the situation, this woman

240

was left with little. And like other destitute widows, she had no job, no home, and no money, left to exist off the kindness of strangers and the generosity of the wealthy.

But for this widow, the most humiliating experience was taking her offering to the temple. There may have been a time when she and her husband had plenty to give. But now the tables had turned. After her husband's death, she was lucky to be able to give even two small copper coins worth about one-half a penny.

Some people would say, "Why bother? Who would miss two little coins? Why take pennies to church? What a worthless gift!"

For this woman, though, giving was not about the amount, it was about the act. Her spirit of generosity was not a reflection of how much she gave, but why she gave. And this is why Jesus noticed her.

The Man Who Invests in Undervalued Assets

Jesus watched intently as the offerings were carried into the temple. There was a pecking order to this extravaganza. Mark and Luke laid out the order for us when they put the "rich people" and their gifts at the head of the line.

If you were bringing a large gift, you would make quite a spectacle of yourself—head turning, big smile, acknowledging the pointing fingers and whispers: "Just look at Mr. Smith. What a gift!" And, most likely, the priest came right over to pat you on the back and assure you that God was indeed on "your side." Why? Because wealth was seen as a blessing of God. Poverty was his curse. If you had only pennies to bring to the church coffers, here's my advice: "In and out fast, and don't make eye contact with anyone."

However, one silent observer was scanning the faces. And if you are an astute investor who identifies a valuable asset, you'll tell others about it—which is just what Jesus did.

241

"Did you see how much the last person gave?" he asked his disciples. Most likely they had not; who would? Such a small gift never got noticed.

Jesus continued with this shocking announcement: "The plain truth is that this widow has given by far the largest offering today. All these others made offerings that they'll never miss; she gave extravagantly what she couldn't afford—she gave her all!" (Luke 21:1–3 Message).

And there it is—Jesus's message on what is valuable and what is not. It's based on this simple rule: you give all, or you give nothing. Those two pennies in and of themselves were absolutely worthless. You could not even have bought a loaf of bread with those coins. But in the hand of a generous heart, those two coins were worth everything because their value was directly related to the person who gave them—a person who did not give from plenty but from poverty, a person who gave everything rather than anything.

You see, what made this woman so valuable to Jesus wasn't her gift. Her value was directly related to what he would be willing to pay for her—and he knew he would give everything for her, just as she had given everything to him—even if it meant giving up his own life. He would give her that much, for she was his priceless treasure!

Our Need—His Response

A penniless widow was worth everything to Jesus. Does that knowledge change the way you look at yourself?

It doesn't matter what we bring to Jesus, how much we have or don't have. We can't bring a bag of gold and make him love us more because his love isn't for sale! I can't put on a fancy pair of shoes or custom suit and get his attention any faster, for the prophet Isaiah said that everything I do to pretty myself up is like covering myself with "grease-stained rags" (Isa. 64:6 Message).

Instead, like the poor widow, I can come with what I have—small as it may be. And the man who invests in undervalued assets stands ready to purchase me with his life. For this is the price he has set for you. That is what you are worth to him. "The Son of Man did not come to be served, but to serve, and to give his life as a ransom for [you]" (Matt. 20:28 NKJV).

His life for yours. His life for mine. That makes us priceless!

> Strive not to be a success, but rather to be of value.
>
> Albert Einstein, physicist

> It is the heart that makes a man [woman] rich. He [she] is rich according to what he [she] is . . . not according to what he [she] has.
>
> Henry Ward Beecher

> I wonder if the day will ever come when a full heart and a full head will count as much as a full purse.
>
> Alfred A. Montapert

A Time for Reflection

The Worthless Woman: A Widow with Two Coins
Background Texts: Mark 12:42–44; Luke 21:1–4

Exploration

My thoughts on feeling worthless . . .

1. What criteria do I use to measure my value?

2. Have I ever felt that because I had less than someone else, I was not as valuable?

Why did I feel this way?

243

3. Are there any "things" I use to measure my self-worth?
What are those "things"?
Why do I think those "things" are of value to me?

Money is not required to buy one necessity of the soul.

Henry David Thoreau

Inspiration

What's the price of two or three pet canaries? Some loose change, right? But God never overlooks a single one. And he pays even greater attention to you, down to the last detail— even numbering the hairs of your head! So don't be intimidated . . . you're worth more than a million canaries.

Luke 12:6–7 Message

Part of my morning routine includes laying out a buffet of safflower, niger thistle, and sunflower seeds for my bird friends. Within minutes of filling a variety of feeders, the blue jays and robins, towhees and titmice, blue birds and cardinals all swoop in to avail themselves of "breakfast." Long after these bigger, brighter birds have gotten their fill and taken flight, the little sparrows and house finches stay behind, seemingly satisfied with the leftovers as they sing like a trained choir.

I like to watch my feathered friends. There's nothing more beautiful than a radiant flock of blue birds sweeping across the sky or a red plumed cardinal flying in and landing on the railing by my kitchen window.

However, of all the delights I am treated to by my bird friends, it is the songs of the sparrows and house finches, both common, unassuming little birds, that bring me the most pleasure.

While I love to see the brightly colored birds, I love most to hear the songs of the common birds—the feathered wonders who would be completely overlooked if it weren't for the joyous melodies they share. They may be small, unnotice-

244

able creatures, but their contribution to the world is immeasurable. Perhaps this is why Jesus likened our value to the sparrows. When you feel overlooked and undervalued, think of the worth given to little birds by your heavenly Father. Remember, your joyous contribution, even if you think it is apparently insignificant, carries an immense value to Jesus.

Use the talents you have; the woods would have little music if no birds sang their song except those who sang best.

Reverend Oliver G. Wilson

1. How do I judge the "worth" of others around me?

2. Do I measure their value by the material things they possess?

3. I am valuable because

4. If I were in the crowd at the temple and were one of the "rich" people bringing a gift, how would I have felt about Jesus's words?

5. If I were in the crowd at the temple and were one of the "poor" people, how would I have felt?

6. What is the "asking price" you would put on something you paid for with your own life?

Affirmation

Are you penniless? Come anyway—buy and eat! Come . . . buy without money—everything's free! Why do you spend your money on junk food, your hard-earned cash on cotton candy? Listen . . . fill yourself with only the finest . . . listen carefully to my life-giving, life-nourishing words.

Isaiah 55:1–3 Message

Compromise *(k˘um'pro-miz')* n.

1. *To settle by concession to something that is harmful or depreciative.*
2. *To give up one's allegiance.*

18

The Compromised Woman

Also, while Pilate was seated on the judgment bench, his wife sent him a message, saying, "Have nothing to do with that just and upright Man, for I have had a painful experience today in a dream because of Him."

Matthew 27:19 AMP

Most everyone has a distinct memory of time spent in school, a recollection that leaves an indelible mark on your life. You may recall a favorite teacher who opened up a world of knowledge, or perhaps you met someone who has become a lifelong friend or even your mate. Whatever the event or whoever the person, memories have a way of serving as guideposts that give us direction the rest of our lives.

When I remember elementary school, there is one incident that sticks in my mind because it eclipses all others, for it taught me a lot about myself. The situation occurred when

I shall be telling this with a sigh somewhere ages and ages hence: two roads diverged in a wood, and I took the one less traveled by, and that has made all the difference.

Robert Frost,
The Poetry of Robert Frost

I was still in fourth grade, but I remember it as though it happened yesterday.

It was a traumatic year. My dad had a job change in the middle of the school year. And while my parents were busy getting ready for a big move, I was experiencing the anxiety kids go through when leaving one group of friends and facing the challenge of trying to fit in with new friends in an unknown town and school.

If I had really liked my teacher that year, things might have been easier, but I didn't. And neither did many of my classmates.

Regrettably, kids can be cruel, not only to each other, but to adults as well. Our teacher, "Mr. M.," became the target of some nasty pranks, most of which took place when his back was turned. The ringleader of our "brat-pack" was a cute guy who was popular and smart. He had all of us eating out of his hand. His wish was our command. Like sheep we followed his orders.

For several weeks, our fearless leader laid out a new scheme each day designed to create classroom havoc. One by one every person in our little group was assigned to carry out some shenanigan that he hatched up.

When my turn arrived, I was commissioned to sneak into the building during recess and write "Mr. M. is stupid" on the chalkboard and on papers that were scattered across his desk. Dutifully I carried out my responsibility.

There was only one problem. As I was leaving the classroom, "Mr. M." came around the corner of the building. He didn't actually see me writing anything, but I had a pretty good idea he got the drift who the culprit was this time.

After recess, when everyone was back at their desks, "Mr. M." called out my name and ordered me to the front of the room. With all eyes in my direction, he asked if I had written the derogatory message on the board, or did I know who had.

I felt forty eyes boring in on me like a laser. The class leader gave me the evil eye as if to say, "If you rat me out I'll do the same to you."

I looked directly at the teacher, and with a poker face, said loud enough for everyone to hear, "I had nothing to do with this. I didn't write on the chalkboard." I then went further: "If you looked at it real good," I noted, "that handwriting doesn't even look like mine."

Needless to say, I know the teacher did not believe me, but without hard evidence to counteract my denial he dropped the issue, and I was told to go back to my desk.

Of course the lie was heralded as a triumph, and my stature among my friends rose tremendously. I was a momentary hero. I had not only saved my neck but my friends' as well!

But after I got home from school I had time to think about my behavior and I was ashamed of myself—hoping my parents never found out and knowing they would be disappointed if they did. I was not raised to lie. Truthfulness was the pinnacle of virtue in our family. Yet in a weak moment, when my back was to the wall, I chose to compromise the values I had been taught in order to keep myself off the hot seat with my teacher and in the good graces of my friends. It was my choice to go along with the crowd so I could elevate my status, even though it meant lying.

Compromise. Accommodate. Conform.

My childhood experience with peer pressure was only a foretaste of the coercion we adults use as we attempt to get what we want.

If you want to get ahead, you have to get along. That means making concessions, accommodating to fit in with the crowd,

> No trumpets sound when the important decisions of our life are made. Destiny is made known silently.
>
> Agnes de Mille

shading the truth, coloring the facts, or as our politicians often do, putting a "spin" on things. We puff ourselves up, leaving false impressions as we try to reach the elevated level of the individuals we want to influence. And before we know it, we find ourselves in the lamentable position of succumbing to the seduction to compromise.

One of my friends who works as a human resource specialist told me that at least 50 percent of the résumés she receives from job applicants contain falsehoods, attempts to influence prospective employers with tainted information.

I am not implying that all compromise is bad. There are times when it is appropriate to be flexible to the needs of others. But when the standards we live by are cast aside, the consequences can be disastrous.

Many years ago, a close friend was dating a wonderful guy, but he didn't fit into her social circle. Finally, she broke up with her boyfriend and ended up marrying someone whose credentials matched her family's model. After twenty years of misery, my friend's marriage disintegrated. Her so-called perfect life was a sham. She had compromised deeply held spiritual values to marry into the "right" world, where the balance on a bank account and the title behind someone's name was all that mattered.

The temptation to compromise doesn't just dog our steps in our "worldly" endeavors either. Even virtuous activities fall prey to the pressure of conformity. You and I have heard statements like "the ends justify the means"—as if to say, "If the end is good, I can use any means in the world to get to my 'good' purpose." It appears some people have the misplaced idea that it is permissible to lie, cheat, and steal, if in the end, the cause they espouse is virtuous. Jesus never taught this theology.

My dad gave me some good advice a long time ago: "Two wrongs don't make a right." As high and mighty as the result of my activity might be, if I have used deceit to accomplish my goal, virtue escapes the entire endeavor. Just because I pray over a meal of worms doesn't turn it into prime steak!

I know all too well how tough it is to keep a straight-arrow line in a crooked world, especially when so many people are getting ahead by going in a different direction. But that doesn't make a wrong decision right.

During the recent litigation of corporate leaders, I heard people interviewed on TV say, "Well, everybody was doing it." That reason determined how their decisions were made. It was the standard by which they measured their own personal behavior. "I'll see what Sally is doing. Then I'll do the same. If she can get away with it, so can I."

There you have it. "Everybody's doing it," the subtitle to compromise, the lure that reels in its victims, dragging us along with the crowd.

To be frank, that line didn't work with my parents when I was a kid, and it doesn't work now as an adult. Blaming someone else for my moral failure only underlines my lack of responsibility for bankrupt behavior.

If, like myself, you have ever yielded to the pressure to compromise, then I believe you will find the experience of Claudia Procula instructive. If ever there was a woman who can teach us that the road to compromise is a slippery slope pointed straight down, it is this woman.

Go Along—to Get Along

She was a product of Roman aristocracy, the granddaughter of Caesar Augustus. And it was in her family's social circle that Claudia Procula met Pilate, the man who became her husband.

251

> Fame is a vapor, popularity an accident, riches take wings, those who cheer today will curse tomorrow, only one thing endures . . . character.
>
> Horace Greeley

Procula's path most likely crossed Pilate's when both were quite young since he, too, was from an eminent Roman family. Pilate's early history was filled with tales of slaying innocent rivals in fits of jealousy. Finally, in desperation, his family sent him to Rome where this ruthless young man was deemed to be "useful" to the empire. And here Procula decided to hitch her wagon to Pilate's rising star. His ambition fit into her ambitious world.

Pilate's first assignment was on an island called Pontus, populated with uncivilized people who had never accepted a ruler. Pilate, to everyone's surprise, became a popular leader. He made such a success of the job he was called, after the island, Pontius Pilate.

"From afar, in Jerusalem, King Herod noticed him. He liked his methods and invited him to be his chief justice in Judea. There Pilate amassed enormous power and huge heaps of silver. He was dangerous, clever, brittle, beautiful and cruel," wrote author Ann Wroe in *Pontius Pilate*.[1]

Pilate's money and power kept Procula satisfied—for a while. The combination of the two can be intoxicating. And with "huge heaps of silver" under her husband's control, Procula lacked for nothing in the way of material possessions. Their home was a palace on the sea at Caesarea Philippi. It was a lavish life the two carved out for themselves, living in the lap of luxury.

But their life together was not without turmoil. Pilate may have had power, but he also had enemies, zealots who longed to embarrass and dethrone the Roman ruler.

Soon, Jewish "messiahs" began to pop up with one goal—to liberate their countrymen from the tyranny of Roman injustice. Procula worried about her husband. She was aware there had been attempts on his life. The most recent person to threaten Pilate's authority was a rabble-rouser named Barabbas, who led an insurrection to unseat Pilate, but to no avail. Pilate wanted to make certain Barabbas's fate served as a warning to other so-called "messiahs," so he decided to save the announcement of a "verdict" on Barabbas's crime until Passover—a Jewish holiday. During the festival, Procula came with her husband to Jerusalem. Author Edith Deen described the scene vividly:

> At this time Procula was probably living in the Herodian Palace at Jerusalem, a luxurious abode with an area large enough to accommodate a hundred guests and furnished and adorned with costly objects, including silver and gold vessels for serving. It had large wings built of white marble and rich, mosaic-paved porticoes with columns of many-colored marble. Through them she could see flashing fountains and luxuriant gardens in which cooed flocks of milk-white doves. Because this palace commanded a view of the open spaces of Jerusalem, she no doubt had looked out on the streets and seen the multitudes following Jesus. And she had come to appreciate the kindly ministry of this man and to know of the many wonders He had performed.[2]

On this particular trip, when Jerusalem was brimming with people and activity, Procula's husband, Pilate, chose to take the opportunity to make a spectacle of his zealot troublemaker. But before Pilate could carry out his plan for Barabbas, another Messiah was brought to his court, a Man named Jesus. And this is when two worlds collided. Pilate was backed into a corner, and he didn't like it at all. He was forced to make a decision. And those without any starch in their backbones find it impossible to stand up for anything. Poor, pitiful Pilate. He was a man who was used to following popular opinion to get where he wanted to go. He was a guy who knew how

> Character is the scribe that writes your true biography.
>
> Alfred A. Montapert

to bargain and compromise to get down the road to success. Taking a stand was out of character for him, especially if his decision proved unpopular with the masses.

Enter Procula, a wife who had gone along to get along. She had heard about Jesus. Some traditions say she was even a secret follower. This could have been the case when we think back to the story of Joanna, Herod's steward's wife. It is likely these two women, both navigating the high end of the Roman social circle at the same time, had crossed paths. Joanna had given up everything Procula was hanging on to. Joanna's devotion to Jesus may have been what set Procula to thinking. And she had to come to one conclusion: Jesus was no Barabbas. He was a man who encouraged his friends to "render to Caesar what he was due." He was a man who instructed his followers to love their enemies. No, Procula knew there was something different about Jesus.

For years, she had stood by and kept her mouth shut. For years she had stood by as Pilate climbed the ladder to success. This time things were about to change.

That thing we call a "conscience" began to show signs of life. Procula didn't like the gnawing feeling in the pit of her stomach. Something was eating away at her. It may have been a man's innocence. But like she had done so often in the past, Procula decided to put the mess out of her head. She would go to bed and hope the troubling thoughts would disappear by morning.

However, sleep would not come. Every time her head hit the pillow, she had a dream, a vision of a man being put to death. She saw an innocent man receiving an unjust sentence. She saw her husband condemning an upright man. The inequity of the situation became too much for Procula. It was time to rock the boat. It was time to question her husband's judgment. It was time to think for herself. It was time to stand up for truth.

Hastily, she wrote a note and asked a servant to take it to Pilate. "Have nothing to do with this just and upright man" (Matt. 27:19 AMP). The Message describes her note this way:

"Don't get mixed up in judging this noble man." Jesus was not guilty. Procula believed it. She knew truth when she saw it, and this was the truth.

The Man Who Tells the Truth

Tyranny and truth faced off in a Roman judgment hall. Compromise and consistency played out in the lives of two men whose fates were at a crossroad.

Jesus stood serenely, surrounded by confusion. Pilate paced nervously, tormented by a message, a letter from a wife who finally decided she had compromised enough for one lifetime.

Procula looked at the two men and made a choice. Truth had bored through to her conscience. But unfortunately things didn't turn out the way she had hoped they would. Her weak-kneed husband didn't release Jesus. Instead, Pilate set a guilty man free.

Pilate chose to dance to a tune called "compromise." Barabbas was free—Jesus was condemned to die. And then, as if to send a message to his wife that it wasn't his fault, Pilate asked for a basin of water so he could "wash his hands" of the whole affair (see Matt. 27:24 KJV).

Heartbroken, Procula had a tough weekend ahead—two nights and three days to think about her life, time to reflect on where her choices had taken her, time to regret how she had gone along to get ahead. And all this time, the one man she believed in, the one man she trusted to tell the truth lay buried in a stone-covered grave.

Truth had bitten the dust— that is, until Sunday morning.

If ever there was a time I would have loved to secretly eavesdrop on a conversation, this would have been it. Procula and Pilate are having breakfast,

Never grow a wishbone, daughter, where your backbone should be.

Clementine Paddleford

relieved the weekend festivities will soon be over, hoping their life will get back to normal, thinking their problems are behind them, when all of a sudden there is a pounding on the door—no light tap, but a frantic beating. It is the captain of the guard.

"Pilate, we have a problem!"

You bet there's a problem. Seems a certain stone-hewn grave is empty. A man is missing, and the word on the grapevine is that he is alive and well in Jerusalem.

If ever an event called out for the words "I told you so," this is it. Procula looks at Pilate. Pilate turns away. He can't bring himself to admit he was wrong and she was right—not this time, not ever.

At that moment, Procula knew that when you stand up for truth, you are not disappointed. At that moment, Procula could understand why Joanna could give up everything she once thought important to follow Jesus.

Jesus gave Procula what Pilate could not: he gave her the truth—and the truth set her free (see John 8:32 KJV). Procula found out that when the truth is on your side, you have the strength to stand up for anything and to anyone.

Our Need—His Response

At a moment of crisis, Procula had to make a choice.

Maybe, like her, you have faced a moment of crisis in your life too—a time when you had to make a decision with no conforming, no concessions, and no compromise. And I ask you, did you do the right thing?

"Great occasions do not make heroes or cowards; they simply unveil them to the eyes of men . . . crisis shows us what we have become," notes Bishop Weston.

In our lives we all face situations where we must stand up for what we believe is truth. But if we compromise our beliefs, we will be led in the wrong direction. That is why another definition for the word *compromise* is "endanger." When I have an "I'll just go along" attitude, I endanger more than my life—I endanger my soul.

Procula confronted truth in a Roman courtroom, and she found that compromise puts blinders on our conscience, but truth gives us 20/20 vision.

If you find yourself plagued by the temptation to compromise what you know to be truth, Procula's experience should serve as a lesson book. There is a man who never lies. There is a man who stands for the truth. And he is the man who will give you the strength to stand firmly for what you believe. As the late Senate chaplain Peter Marshall so eloquently prayed, "Give to us clear vision that we may know where to stand and what to stand for—because unless we stand for something, we shall fall for anything."

> May your love and your truth always protect me.
>   Psalm 40:11 NIV

A Time for Reflection

The Compromised Woman: Procula, Pilate's Wife
Background Text: Matthew 27:19

Exploration

My thoughts about compromise . . .

1. When and how have I compromised to get what I want?

2. Why did I compromise?

3. What did I learn from this event?

4. How do I respond to pressure to conform when it goes against what I believe to be truth?

Take heed to yourselves, lest your [mind and] heart
be deceived, and you turn aside and serve other gods
and worship them.

Deuteronomy 11:16 AMP

Courage is coming to realize that what does and does
not happen in the world does so because of what you
and I fail to say—not when silence is right, but when
we fear the cost to ourselves of speaking out.

Joan D. Chittister, *Scarred by Struggle,*
Transformed by Hope

Inspiration

The one thing that doesn't abide by majority rule is a person's
conscience.

Harper Lee, *To Kill a Mockingbird*

Several months ago, my husband and I watched a biography
on the life of the German Lutheran pastor Dietrich Bonhoeffer,
best known as a victim of the Nazi Gestapo. Bonhoeffer, at
the end of World War II, was hanged at the age of thirty-nine
for being involved in a plot to assassinate Adolf Hitler.

During the many months he spent confined to prison, he
wrote regarding his conviction that Christian faith must be
an active faith. Many of his writings, which have been shared
with the world, are filled with his obvious concern, maybe
even an inner battle, to know how far one should go as we
heed the call to obey what we know is truth.

In his *Letters from Prison* he seeks to answer this critical
question, "Who Stands Fast?" Here is his answer:

Only the man whose final standard is not his reason, his prin-
ciples, his conscience, his freedom, or his virtue, but who is
ready to sacrifice all this when he is called to obedient and
responsible action in faith and in exclusive allegiance to God—
the responsible man, who tries to make his whole life an answer
to the question and call of God.[3]

I'd like to personalize the last part of this thoughtful statement: You may wish to insert your name and your commitment in this declaration:

And Jesus began to tell them, be careful and watchful that no one misleads (deceives) you.

Mark 13:5 AMP

Only the responsible woman, Dorothy, who will make her whole life an answer to the question and call of God.

The answer to Dietrich Bonhoeffer's question was played out in a crucifixion drama set in a Roman court. Truth took the stand and prevailed when a privileged Roman princess made the decision to heed the call of Jesus when he said, "Follow me."

1. If I had been in Procula's shoes, what would I have done to convey my belief that Jesus was innocent?

2. What do I think happened in Procula's life after the death of Jesus?

3. What would have happened in my life after Jesus's death if I had been Procula?

4. How have I responded to truth in my life?

Affirmations

[There was a] wise [woman] who built [her] house on a rock. And the rain fell and the floods came and the winds blew and beat against that house; yet it did not fall, because it had been founded on the rock.

Matthew 7:24–25 AMP

Do not follow the crowd in doing wrong.

Exodus 23:2 NIV

Lonely *(lōn'lē)* adj.

1. Unfrequented by people: desolate.

2. Dejected by being alone.

3. Friendless.

19

The Lonely Woman

Jesus saith unto her, "Woman, why weepest thou? Whom seekest thou?" She, supposing him to be the gardener, saith unto him, "Sir, if thou have borne him hence, tell me where thou hast laid him, and I will take him away." Jesus saith unto her, "Mary."

John 20:15–16 KJV

Maybe it was her tousled white hair or irrepressible giggle—whatever it was, I knew I had made a friend the first time I met Hazel. Even though she was forty years older than I, her mischievous sense of adventure led me to believe she was much younger than her eighty years.

It did not take long before I found out we had a shared interest—clothes. Hazel worked for years as a seamstress. Soon she was bringing me old Vogue patterns she had used in the 1950s. Much to her delight I had an outfit made from one of the designs.

Hazel began to spend more time at our home. Every Christmas she would join our family for the holiday festivities. But for all of Hazel's happy laughter and continual chatter, there were just some things she would not talk about. Whenever the mention of family came up in a conversation, Hazel became strangely quiet. You could not get her to talk about her past.

> The body is a house of many windows. There we all sit, showing ourselves and crying on the passerby to come and love us.
>
> Robert Lewis Stevenson

The time came when the small church we attended was planning a party to help us get to know each other in a more personal way. Someone had the idea to ask people how they got their names. We decided we would ask individuals ahead of time, and when I received my list to call, there was Hazel's name.

I phoned and asked if she would participate. "No," she said emphatically. And that was the end of the discussion.

A few weeks later when I saw Hazel she said, "Dorothy, I want you to know how I got my name. May I tell you?" She took a deep breath and the words began to tumble out.

"My parents died when I was just a baby. Back in those days, without family or close friends, kids like me ended up in orphanages. That's where I was put. It wasn't a pleasant place." As she talked, it was obvious the memory still disturbed her.

"By the time I was four or five, I'd given up on ever being adopted. Then one day, when I was seven years old, a man and woman came to the orphanage. They had a list of requirements. They wanted to find a young girl with blue eyes and blond hair. And one more thing: she had to be seven years old. I matched their list perfectly. So they took me home."

The pain on Hazel's face as she related the story caused me to say, "Hazel, if this hurts too much you don't have to continue."

"No. I want to tell you the whole story. When the couple took me to their home I was so happy. It was a big house. They took me upstairs and showed me my own bedroom. It was all fixed up with a bed and beautiful curtains. They opened up the closet, and it was filled with clothes just my size. I had never seen anything like this in my life.

"Then something very strange happened. They told me my name now was to be Hazel, and I was born on a certain day in August. At first I didn't understand what was going on, but soon it all became clear.

"They had a daughter who was seven years old when she died suddenly. Unable to recover from their loss they decided to 'replace' her with me. They gave me her name. They even gave me her birthday.

"You know, Dorothy," she said, as she looked into my eyes and squeezed my hand, "I don't know how old I really am. I can't remember my real birthday. I don't even remember what my name was before I went to live with them. You see, Hazel isn't really my name. Unfortunately, I was never able to replace the real 'Hazel' for these people. I think they always resented me. When I was old enough and things got really bad, I finally ran away." As the tears rolled down Hazel's soft wrinkled face, she grabbed my hands, and with great sadness in her voice, whispered, "Sometimes I feel so alone."

Lonely. Forgotten. Abandoned.

No birthday. No name. No identity. Hazel knew what it was like to feel alone.

How about you? Like Hazel, have you had moments when the fog of loneliness has covered you like a thick blanket and you have been left feeling you didn't matter to anyone?

Loneliness can creep up on us, enveloping us slowly, almost imperceptibly. It can be a nagging pain that haunts us when the lights are turned out, or it can come upon us suddenly like a tornado of terror.

While I have never felt the deep sting of loneliness like Hazel, I am certain each of us can remember a time when we were terrified we had been forgotten, left alone.

I still recall the day I flew by myself for the very first time. I was in my early teens and had convinced my parents to let me visit friends in San Francisco.

They took me to Los Angeles International Airport, and like most concerned moms and dads, they escorted me into the terminal and stayed at the window waving as the plane taxied away.

Just before we landed in San Francisco, the pilot's voice came over the speaker, announcing we would be circling the airport for a while. We could not land because of fog.

A few minutes of circling turned into an hour, then two. Finally, the wheels of the plane touched the runway. By the time I got into the airport, I was late by nearly three hours. To make matters worse, thousands of other passengers faced the same dilemma. There were so many bodies crammed into the terminal it was impossible to move. I scanned the faces, trying desperately to find one I recognized.

After frantic searching, I sat down and tried to compose myself. I looked inside my wallet. There was the money my mom handed me just before I got on the plane. "It's for an emergency, honey," she said as she kissed me good-bye.

Calm down, I kept saying to myself. I tried hard not to think about the stories I had heard of teenage girls alone in big cities. That's when I decided to call home. Hopefully, my parents would be home. Maybe they would know what I should do. I was certain my friends must have left the airport long ago, thinking I had missed the plane or that I was not coming at all.

As I made my way down a long corridor, shoved along by the crush of other bodies, I heard a voice call out above the noise, "Dorothy!" I whirled around and there, standing on a chair above the crowd, was one of my friends.

What a relief—someone was waiting for me! And with one

> Nobody, but nobody can make it out here alone.
>
> Maya Angelou,
> writer and educator

264

word—"Dorothy"—my fears melted. I was not alone and had not been forgotten.

We can be in a terminal filled with people and feel dreadfully alone. We can be orphaned like Hazel, without a lifeline from anyone who cares, and feel alone. We can even live in a house with a family and still feel alone.

During World War II, Anne Frank kept a diary that left a record of the terrifying events she faced. There were days when the thought of being torn away by soldiers overwhelmed her. Her poignant words give a glimpse into the feelings she experienced, even when surrounded by her family: "A person can be lonely even if she is loved by many people because she may not feel she is the one and only to anyone."

In our crowded society filled with traffic jams, long lines, and crowds on every corner, it is still easy to feel alone. We feel disconnected, as though we do not matter.

Researchers have a name for this "crowded" type of loneliness we experience. They call it LTL—Living Together Loneliness.

Ralph Keyes in *We the Lonely People* observes that as Americans, we value our mobility, privacy, and convenience. As a result, it becomes almost impossible for us to develop a deep sense of community.

Over the last fifty years, our society has become even more isolated and disconnected. In the 1950s, only one in ten people lived alone. Now this figure has skyrocketed into one in four. Statistics show that due to death, a high divorce rate, and deferred marriage, by the year 2010 over 31 million Americans will be alone—in a crowded world!

So we search, hunting for people who care, hoping we will not be forgotten, yet fearing that due to circumstances beyond our control we will end up old and all alone.

If you find yourself caught in the clutches of loneliness, you need to meet Mary Magdalene. If ever a person had a reason to feel alone and abandoned, it was Mary.

In the Garden of the Lost and Found

It was dark. Morning light would come soon. Since Mary could not sleep, she crept through the darkness all by herself, down a rocky dirt path, making her way to a garden.

Mary came to this spot because she didn't know what else to do or where else to go. In just a few short days her world had been turned upside down. The life she had grown to love had been destroyed.

Terror seized Mary as she made her way to the garden. Memories from the past flooded her mind—haunting memories filled with the remembrance of desperate days and nights. Seven times she had lost her mind. Some doctors claimed she had seven personalities. Dr. Luke, one of Jesus's disciples, reported she was possessed by "seven devils" (see Luke 8:2). Whatever plagued Mary, it was persistent. The problem didn't go away on its own. For years her life was filled with insanity. Then she met Jesus.

There was no doubt he had pulled her from the abyss. When her family and friends had given up on her, Jesus did not.

Mary had pinned her hopes and future on Jesus. He had given her a new mind and a new life. As long as he was around, she felt safe and free. But now he was gone, and the chains of the past tightened their grip on her. Fear clutched at Mary's heart. What if she got sick . . . again? What if her mind played tricks on her . . . again? What if the demons plagued her . . . again? What would she do? Suddenly, feelings she had forgotten came rushing over her like a tidal wave—fear, loss, and loneliness.

The Man Who Never Forgets

Alone in a garden, Mary Magdalene stood weeping. A helpful gardener approached, trying to comfort the grief-stricken woman.

"Why are you crying? Who are you looking for?"

Mary was so absorbed in her own world she didn't recognize the face. Nor did she recognize the voice, until she heard the one thing she longed to hear more than anything else in the world.

"Mary."

Over her sobs, drowning out the tumult of the last few days, piercing the pain of loneliness that ripped her heart in pieces, Mary heard Jesus call her by name. All it took was one word. And she knew she was not alone. Jesus had not forgotten her.

On that day the man who knows each of us personally stopped the universe for one brief moment, adjusted his schedule, and told his Father that there was a little matter he must take care of before returning home. He wanted to visit a garden to tell his dear friend he would never forget her.

Jesus had not forgotten how traumatic Mary's life had been. And so, to protect her, rather than come to the garden as a soldier or a heavenly being, Jesus came as an unassuming gardener. Someone who was familiar. Someone Mary would expect to see in a garden early in the morning. Someone who would not frighten her.

Jesus had not forgotten how others talked about Mary. I can imagine she was the hot topic of discussion back in her hometown of Magdala. "Remember the nut case, the girl possessed by evil spirits? I was so relieved when she left town." People had gossiped about Mary for years. But when she met Jesus the whispering began to stop. Jesus treated her with such respect that soon Mary began to notice other people treated her respectfully, also. Jesus came to the garden that morning to send a message to Mary's critics: "There's no such thing as a 'hopeless case.'"

Jesus had not forgotten how much Mary depended on him. He could not leave Mary without letting her know she could continue to count on him. His love for her was a "never let you go" type of love. She could trust him to be there for her every day of her life. Just because he was out of her sight did not mean she was out of his thoughts.

Most importantly Jesus had not forgotten Mary's name. She was not part of a crowd or a number on a census bureau sheet. She had a name—a name he would never forget, no matter where she was or where he went.

Our Need—His Response

Do you feel alone? Forgotten? Abandoned? Left to make your way by yourself? Has the lifeline you held onto been wrenched from your hand, leaving you to flounder in the sea of life? And now waves of bitter loneliness are crashing over you, threatening to sink you.

If you feel you have been left to battle the tempest by yourself, Jesus wants you to know he did not forget Mary— and he has not forgotten you. If a woman everyone else had given up on was worth Jesus's time and attention, you are too.

Jesus could easily have left a message for Mary with one of her friends, or he could have had an angel deliver words of comfort. Instead, he knew the only way he could assure Mary that she would always be in his thoughts was to tell her personally. Heaven could wait while he remembered a friend in need.

But what's more, Jesus asked Mary to deliver a message to his disciples. "Go to my brethren, and say unto them, I ascend unto my Father, and your Father; and to my God, and your God" (John 20:17 KJV).

No longer was Mary Magdalene the lonely, desperate figure weeping in the garden. A visit from Jesus transformed her into a courageous messenger, the bearer of the greatest news bulletin ever heralded on planet Earth: "He is risen!"

You can be confident with the knowledge that what Jesus did for Mary, he will do for you. You matter to him—not as a faceless, nameless person, but as a distinct individual he will never forget. He remembers every detail about you right down to the number of hairs on your head. "Even the very hairs of your head are all numbered. So don't be afraid" (Matt. 10:30–31 NIV). He has promised he will never forget us, whether we are called Hazel, Mary Magdalene, or even if we have a name we cannot remember.

> We live in a society in which loneliness has become one of the most painful wounds. The growing competition and rivalry which pervade our lives . . . have created in us an acute awareness of our isolation.
>
> Henri J. M. Nouwen, *The Wounded Healer*

A Time for Reflection

The Lonely Woman: Mary Magdalene
Background Texts: Matthew 27:56, 61; 28:1; Mark 15:40, 47; 16:1, 9; Luke 8:2; 24:10; John 19:25; 20:1–18

Exploration

My thoughts on loneliness . . .

1. Is there a time in my life when I felt alone? What was that time?

2. What words describe my feelings when I am alone?

3. Do I fear being left alone when:
   A. I leave home for the first time? (Explain)
   B. Someone I love dies? (Explain)
   C. I grow old? (Explain)

269

4. What methods have I used in the past to get through a time of loneliness?

> When souls really touch, it is forever. Then space and time disappears, and all that remains is the consciousness that we are not alone in life.
>
> Joan Chittister

Inspiration

> I come to the garden alone while the dew is still on the roses; and the voice I hear, falling on my ear, the Son of God discloses. And He walks with me, and He talks with me. And He tells me I am His own; and the joy we share as we tarry there, none other has ever known.
>
> "In the Garden,"
> words by C. Austin Miles,
> 1912, public domain

1. What lessons can I learn from Jesus's visit with Mary Magdalene in the garden?

2. Has someone helped me through a time of loneliness?
   Who was the person?
   What did they do for me?

3. How will I respond to the fear of being left alone in the future?

4. Who is the someone in my life who needs me to tell them they are not forgotten?

> I will not in any way fail you nor give you up nor leave you without support. I will not in any degree leave you helpless nor let you down. Assuredly not!
>
> Hebrews 13:5 AMP

Affirmations

Can a mother forget the baby at her breast and have no compassion on the child she has borne? Though she may forget, I will not forget you! See, I have engraved you on the palms of my hands.

Isaiah 49:15–16 NIV

Lonely? No not lonely while Jesus standeth by; His presence always cheers me, I know that He is nigh. Friendless? No not friendless, for Jesus is my friend; I change, but He remaineth, the same unto the end. No, never alone, no never alone, He has promised never to leave me, never to leave me alone.

"Lonely, Never Lonely," words by J.C.H. and V.A.
White, public domain

Transformed *(trans-fôrm'd)*

1. To change the form or outward appearance of.
2. To change the condition, nature, or function of; convert.
3. To change the personality or character of.

20

The Transformed Women

Wait and listen, everyone who is thirsty! Come to the waters
and [she] who has no money, come, buy, and eat! Yes, come,
buy priceless spiritual wine and milk without money and
without price simply for the self-surrender that accepts the
blessing . . .

Isaiah 55:1 AMP

The physical therapist assigned to my case came into the room
at the rehabilitation hospital where my husband, Jim, and I
had been recuperating for several months after our auto accident. He picked up the slide board I used to navigate from
the bed to the wheelchair.

"Get into your chair, Dorothy," the therapist said with a
grin. "You're going for a ride."

Within minutes he had transported me downstairs to the
hospital gym where he pushed my wheelchair up to a set of
parallel bars.

"Today, you are going to stand up," he announced. "The doctor has given us the go-ahead to let you begin to bear weight on your legs."

With a physical therapist on either side assisting and encouraging me, I stood upright for the first time in months. For forty-five seconds, which seemed like an eternity, my shaky legs brought me to a vertical position. And then I fell back into the safety of my chair. I didn't want to stay in the chair for the rest of my life. I wanted to walk again. But having to face the trauma of standing on legs and feet that were fractured and painful was a terrifying experience. I was certain my wobbly legs and disfigured feet could never hold me up. How could legs that were so injured ever heal enough to make it possible for me to walk as I had in the past?

Again and again over the next few weeks, I tried to stand with the help of the parallel bars. After numerous attempts, I began to navigate the length of the bars one slow step at a time. This accomplishment gave me the incentive to try even harder. Next I was fitted with a walker that had a special "shelf" for my broken left arm. With a therapist behind me pushing a wheelchair in case I needed to sit down, I began to walk around the gym, an environment where I felt safe and secure.

My next hurdle was to attempt to walk down the hospital hallway. The first effort was a catastrophe. I felt as though I would faint. Fortunately, by grabbing the rail on the wall, I was able to let myself down onto the floor, and the therapist quickly got me back into my wheelchair—my security blanket.

It wasn't long, however, before a few feet became a five-minute walk, then a fifteen-minute walk. And before I knew it, I could actually walk on a treadmill for thirty minutes at a time.

My wounds were healing. My broken bones were mending. Legs that trembled became stable. Muscles that were flaccid developed strength. Every day, imperceptibly at first, I began to navigate with less pain and greater ease.

Transformed. Reborn. Metamorphosed.

Several years later, as I look back on the experience of watching my broken body, held together with bolts, screws, and metal wires, heal, I find myself amazed at the transformation that has taken place.

Most of the time I didn't even realize the healing process was occurring. Then, all of a sudden, one day I was able to do some task I once could not accomplish. I could stand longer, walk farther, lift more. What was once difficult became easy. The impossible became possible.

In your life and mine, bones are not the only things that get broken. Our physical body is not all that gets fractured. Promises are broken. Relationships are fractured. A spirit is crushed. Hopes are dashed to pieces. And dreams are destroyed.

The result is that we find ourselves shattered, not only physically but emotionally and spiritually. Our emotions may be in shreds, scarred by toxic relationships. Our spirituality may be betrayed by a religion that left us covered in guilt rather than grace.

If there is a part of your life that is broken, I hope you have been able to identify with one of the women we have come to know in the pages of this book. Together we have become acquainted with a group of ladies who are now our soul sisters, friends, companions, and role models.

These are not women whose lives mirrored fantasy rather than fact. These ladies are the real thing. We cannot reduce their lives to small framed pictures on a mantle or icons on a shelf. To do so would be to discard the value their lives give to you and me.

As we have been witness to their struggles portrayed in

> God's . . . gracious Word can make you into what he wants you to be and give you everything you could possibly need.
>
> Acts 20:32 Message

275

"living color," we have come to know them "up close and personal." We have found they did not live charmed lives. We have seen their mistakes. We have also experienced their victories. And this is why their stories contain such meaning.

These were not women who had it all figured out. They weren't little "Miss Perfects" who never made a mistake. No, these were real girls with real problems trying to balance family and work, illness and health, poverty and prosperity.

Their culture may have been different from ours, but their struggles were the same. They faced the same obstacles you and I do, just at a different time and in a different place.

As I have become familiar with each of these women, I have come to realize they wanted the same things I want. Each woman had a heart that craved love. They wanted to feel complete, whole, healed. And in the end they wanted ultimate fulfillment. Isn't that what you want too?

But like so many of us, their paths detoured into uncharted territory. They tried to fill up the empty spaces in their lives with material possessions, or they chased after a "you can do it yourself" philosophy. Most of these women ended up trying to find healing in all the wrong places.

You and I have been there, done that. Like these women we have tried to fix what is broken by polishing the outside rather than healing the inside. It is a technique that has not worked for me, and it may not have worked for you.

These women couldn't fix themselves, and you and I can't either. They tried on their own to climb the mountains, but they found them too high. They tried leaping the hurdles, but they were too far apart. The challenges they faced pushed them beyond their capability. Life has a way of doing that to every one of us.

And so these women decided to seek help—not some here-today, gone-tomorrow, quick-fix remedy. No, they went out on a limb for the real deal.

They bought into the truth as presented by a man folks scoffed at and called a phony Messiah. They chose to believe in a guy who confronted them with the issues that tormented their lives. These bold women said "yes" to Jesus's method of human repair—a personal intervention. And much to their surprise, a transformation began to take place in their lives.

Fantasy Meets Reality

Just look back with me at how these women's lives were changed.

A pregnant peasant girl became the mother of the man who has affected history more than any other person in the world. She taught us that perfection doesn't mean you are flawless; it means you do the best you can with what you have been given.

An elderly, childless widow found that it only takes open arms to fill an empty heart. And what's more, she let us in on a little secret: you can have children at any age.

Then there was the rejected girl who found out we all have family who love and accept us, warts and all. A socialite, born into wealth, living in luxury, willingly traded in the rich life and, in the process, gained eternal life.

An insecure mother-in-law showed us we have a solid rock under our feet. An isolated woman was able to teach us we are safe to experience the warmth of human touch. And a dead child who was given life for her soul showed us that helping hands can bring life to hungry bodies.

Worried mothers had their troubled hearts soothed by a hand of peace and their burdens lifted by a hand of strength.

An ignored woman found someone who listened. A labeled woman was given a name she loved. A grieving woman found hope is alive and well. A sinful woman was able to grasp the certainty she was covered by grace, not condemned by guilt.

A stressed-out woman found rest. A misunderstood woman finally found a Man who understood her heart. An ambitious woman found success wasn't climbing over but lifting up. A worthless woman learned value isn't measured by dollars and cents. A woman who had sold her soul to compromise found truth at last. And a lonely woman discovered we are never forgotten.

The Man Who Transforms Us

Minute by minute, day by day, each of these women began to experience a change in herself. Lives that were in tatters were woven into patterns of beauty. Crushed dreams were resurrected, broken hearts mended.

The women we met, however, did not get to the point of transformation by reading self-help books or following the latest advice fad. Each woman began the healing process when she met Jesus. He was different from anyone they had ever known. He accepted them as they were, inspired them to be more, challenged them as they moved forward, and guided them to a new future.

It is no wonder the women became Jesus's best friends, his financial supporters, his encouragers, and his defenders. When three of Jesus's disciples pooped out—the ladies stayed awake. When Jesus's disciples hid out, the women stayed by his side. And when Judas took himself out, the ladies still followed.

The love that drew these women to Jesus in the first place became the glue that held them together in the last place. And that last place was a grave in a garden where they went in the dark of night to care for the dead body of the Man they loved.

When Jesus was betrayed by a friend, arrested like a common criminal, and hauled off to Pilate's court, the women kept following—not in the shadows, but right out in public, in full view for everyone to see.

They watched in horror as a Roman soldier's whip slashed Jesus's back. Tears rolled down their cheeks as he groaned when a crown of thorns was jammed into the flesh on his scalp. As spikes were driven through his loving hands, the scene became too painful for them to watch. But they would not leave. They wanted to know if this man was for real. Would he keep his word? Was he the one he said he was? Was his love what they really had been searching for?

Jesus had done so much for them. He had given them health, purpose, value, and love. He had given them something to hope for and someone to believe in. These girls didn't go to a lonely tomb in the dark of night to satisfy their curiosity. They went there to verify their belief. This wasn't a show of women's intuition; it was the reality of women's conviction.

Forget that thieves haunted the rocky terrain outside the gates of Jerusalem. Ignore the fact that over one hundred Roman soldiers had been commanded to guard the grave where Jesus's body lay. These women would brave the cold, the dark, and the threat of bodily harm to get to the man they had come to love.

As they walked in the darkness, their conversation turned to Jesus. Joanna reminded everyone of how Jesus had healed her of a terminal disease. Next it was Mary Magdalene's turn. People thought she was a hopeless case—except Jesus. One by one each woman told a story, a story of what Jesus's love had done for her. By the time they had finished, hope began to build in each heart.

"Jesus said he would rise in three days," exclaimed Joanna. "Do you believe it could happen?" (see Matt. 12:40).

"I do. I do. I do." One voice after another affirmed the belief that indeed Jesus was who he said he was.

Their feet moved faster. Today was day number three. Could it be possible? They were nearly running. In their hearts they knew something was going to happen.

Ahead they saw the grave that held the body of their friend. Gone were the soldiers. No rock covered the tomb. Something was wrong with this picture. No, on second thought, everything was right with this picture. "He is not here, for he is risen" (see Mark 16:4–6). A personal message delivered to the women by angelic messengers left behind to convey heaven's good news to hearts that loved Jesus—to women who believed in him.

The women had followed Jesus. They trusted him. They loved him. And Jesus loved them in return. That is why he would not leave their company without a farewell message.

And this is the "love note" he left behind:

"My love is constant . . . I will never give up on you. My love will weather every storm . . . I will never change. My love conquers mountains . . . I am strong. My love reaches down . . . I will lift you up. My love is forever . . . I will never let you go."

Our Need—His Response

What a group, these girls from Galilee, the women of Judea and Samaria. Flawed. Empty. Rejected. Unfulfilled. Insecure. Isolated. Hungry. Worried. Ignored. Labeled. Hopeless. Guilty. Stressed. Misunderstood. Ambitious. Worthless. Compromised. Lonely. It isn't what you or I would call a "Power Team"!

But these women found that a friendship with one man changed all that. Just when they thought they would end up with Mr. Wrong, they found Mr. Right. All the heavy baggage that weighed them down was thrown overboard. All the painful scars that reminded them of their past failures were transformed into beauty marks.

Over the last few years, as I have watched my broken bones heal and my scars fade, I have been reminded that what was once weak can become strong. The scars on my body don't remind me of old injuries but of new life.

If you feel shattered and scarred, there is healing for your broken places. And soon the ugly blemishes that once reminded you of your failures and marred the beauty in your soul will serve as trophies of your renewed strength and wholeness.

The good news is this healing doesn't come at a high price. You don't have to mortgage your future to pay for transformation now. "And so we are transfigured . . . our lives gradually becoming brighter and more beautiful as God enters our lives and we become like him" (2 Cor. 3:18 Message). The change is happening—a gift to you from Jesus— the man who loves and transforms you. "For God so loved the world that he gave his only begotten Son, that whosoever believeth in Him, should not perish but have everlasting life" (John 3:16 KJV).

> Love never fails, never fades out or becomes obsolete or comes to an end.
>
> 1 Corinthians 13:8 AMP

A Time for Reflection

> The Lord is my guide. I shall not lack . . . He refreshes and restores my life.
>
> Psalm 23:1, 3 AMP

Exploration

My thoughts on being transformed . . .

1. If I could change my life, what single thing would I alter?
   Why?

2. How have I tried to change my life?
   Have I been successful in trying to change my life on my own?

281

3. What challenges have I encountered trying to fix things myself?

4. Where have I turned to get the help I need?

> You have made us for yourself and our souls find no rest until they find it in you.
>
> St. Augustine

> Being confident of this, that he who began a good work in you will carry it on to completion.
>
> Philippians 1:6 NIV

Inspiration

A number of years ago, the company I worked for was hired to assist Teen Challenge in Southern California with some of their fund-raising activities. I was delighted when the executive director invited me to visit all their facilities. At the time, the Teen Challenge residential program housed, on a full-time basis, both men and women in different locations from Bakersfield to Ventura to Riverside, California. The heart of their program was to assist individuals with drug abuse problems in their effort to not only "kick their habit" but find a permanent, spiritual change through Christ that would transform their lives.

The house where the women resided in Ventura, California, was a large frame home—a Victorian-style house with a large number of bedrooms. Obviously, because it was an older building, the kitchen did not contain many of the modern conveniences we have all come to rely on. There was no dishwasher, no garbage disposal, and no microwave oven.

As I walked through the house, I was drawn to the kitchen where several of the girls were doing dishes the old-fashioned way—soap and sink, and towels for drying. When I entered the kitchen there was a "hum" of voices speaking, and at first I thought I must be walking in on a discussion. But closer listening and observation revealed the what and why of the girls' activity.

Taped to the old, white backsplash tile behind the sink were small slips of paper with handwritten notes on them. Upon closer scrutiny I could see that the words were texts of Scripture. As the girls went about their daily activities, they repeated these texts until they had memorized them.

Later I was able to sit down with several of the girls and ask them questions one-on-one. I asked the first young lady I spoke with about the kitchen routine. She smiled and said, "Well, it's like this. Over the years many of us have had people tell us how worthless we are, and soon we came to believe it. I found my mind was filled with many negative thoughts, but now I am filling my mind with something positive. I am replacing the bad thoughts with good ones."

And then I asked her this question: "Has it made a difference?"

There was no hesitation in her response. "You can't believe the change. I am a totally different person than I was just a few months ago."

A Native American tale tells of the elder who was talking to a disciple. The elder said, "I feel as if I have two wolves fighting in my heart. One wolf is the vengeful, angry, violent one. The other wolf is the loving compassionate one." The disciple asked, "But which wolf will win the fight in your heart?" And the holy one answered, "It depends on which one I feed."

The apostle Paul, writing to his friends in Rome, encouraged them with this advice: "Do not conform any longer to the pattern of this world, but be transformed by the renewing of your mind" (Rom. 12:2 NIV). I like the way this text reads in the Message. "Don't become so well-adjusted to your culture that you fit into it without even thinking. Instead, fix your attention on God. You'll be changed from the inside out" (Rom. 12:2 Message). And what is the result of focusing our attention on God who wants to transform us? Paul goes on to write, "Then you will be able to test and approve what God's will is." We will know God's will, for we will be walking in his way.

See that you go on growing in the Lord, and become strong and vigorous in the truth.

Colossians 2:7 TLB

1. What does it mean to be "renewed" in 2 Corinthians 4:15–16 (AMP), or as it reads in the Greek New Testament, "renovated"?

2. In what ways did Jesus transform the women who were his friends?

3. What specific area in my life needs the restoring touch of Jesus?

4. Like the women we've met, how do I believe Jesus can change my life? (See John 3:5–8 NIV and Message.)

5. Will I let fear keep me from change?

That which we love, we come to resemble.
St. Bernard of Clairvaux (1091–1153)

Affirmations

On the next few pages are twenty affirmations, or, as my husband Jim's Cuban family would say, "afirmaciŏnes." I like the rich Spanish translation—"a declaration."

I found out just how important declaring something is when several years ago I attended a seminar designed especially for women who wanted to start their own businesses. At the end of the day after group sessions, we were all invited into a large auditorium where the leader asked the crowd of over three hundred to do three things.

First, she asked us to take a sheet of unused paper and write down the single goal we wanted to accomplish with our business plan during the upcoming twelve months. After we finished she asked us to read that goal to the person sitting next to us. And finally, she invited brave souls in the room to come up front and tell the entire group what they were going to do. Why? Because she said, "Those of you who do these three things here today have an 80 percent or greater chance of doing what you have said because you have declared to us what you will do."

The same goes for you and me when we not only read but testify to the transformation in our lives. I declare. I testify. I speak. But there's one big difference. We aren't forming a business. We're developing a relationship with a man who promises, "I will never slumber or sleep . . . I will keep your life" (see Ps. 121:3, 7). He is on-the-job 365 days a year, twenty-four hours a day, transforming us with his power. And his track record is not 80 percent—it is 100 percent. Or as the prophet Jeremiah once wrote, "His love never fails, it is new every day" (see Lam. 3:22–23).

This promise is not in the past tense or looking ahead to some future time. It is spoken in the present. What is transpiring, though I may not always recognize it, is happening now. A new life is yours and mine today!

It is my prayer that these affirmations will become part of the fabric of the beautiful life God has for you.

> Take on an entirely new way of life—a God-fashioned life renewed from the inside.
>
> Ephesians 4:23 Message

Daily Declarations

> Other books were given for our information, the Bible was given for our transformation.
>
> Anonymous

When a Woman Meets Jesus

1. From Broken to Whole

"May God himself, the God who makes everything holy and whole, make you holy and whole, put you together—spirit, soul, and body . . . the One who called you is completely dependable. If he said it, he'll do it!" (1 Thess. 5:23–24 Message).

2. From Flawed to Perfected

"God is love, and He who dwells and continues in love dwells and continues in God and God dwells and continues in him. In this communion love is brought to completion and attains perfection" (1 John 4:16–17 AMP).

3. From Empty to Full

"I will always show you where to go. I'll give you a full life in the emptiest of places . . . you'll be like a well-watered garden, a gurgling spring that never runs dry" (Isa. 58:11 Message).

4. From Rejected to Accepted

"To the praise of the glory of his grace, wherein he hath made us accepted in the beloved" (Eph. 1:6 KJV).

5. From Unfulfilled to Satisfied

"O satisfy us with Your mercy, and loving-kindness . . . that we may rejoice and be glad all our days" (Ps. 90:14 AMP).

"Oh, that [women] would praise and confess to the Lord for His goodness and loving-kindness and His wonderful works . . . for He satisfies the longing soul and fills the hungry soul with good" (Ps. 107:8–9 AMP).

6. From Insecure to Settled

"I waited patiently for the Lord; and he inclined unto me and heard my cry. He brought me out of a horrible pit, out of the miry clay, and set my feet upon a rock" (Ps. 40:1–3 KJV).

7. From Isolated to Liberated

"The spirit of the Lord God is upon me, because the Lord has anointed and qualified me to preach the Gospel of good

286

tidings to the meek, to the poor, and afflicted; He has sent me to bind up and heal the brokenhearted, to proclaim liberty to the captives" (Isa. 61:1 AMP).

"Now the Lord is the spirit, and where the spirit of the Lord is, there is freedom" (2 Cor. 3:17 NIV).

8. From Hungry to Filled

"Blessed are those who hunger and thirst for righteousness, for they will be filled" (Matt. 5:6 NIV).

"You're blessed when you've worked up a good appetite for God. His food and drink is the best meal you'll ever eat" (Matt. 5:6 Message).

9. From Worried to Contented

"And God's peace shall be yours, that tranquil state of a soul assured of its salvation through Christ, and so fearing nothing from God and being content with its earthly lot of whatever sort that is, that peace which transcends all understanding shall garrison and mount guard over your hearts and minds in Christ Jesus" (Phil. 4:7 AMP).

10. From Ignored to Esteemed

"What marvelous love the Father has extended to us! Just look at it—we're called children of God! That's who we really are!" (1 John 3:1–2 Message).

11. From Labeled to Honored

"The Lord God is my strength and he will make my feet like [a deer's] feet and he will make me walk on high places" (Hab. 3:19 KJV).

12. From Hopeless to Expectant

"My soul, wait only upon God and silently submit to Him; for my hope and expectation are from Him" (Ps. 62:5 AMP).

13. From Guilty to Blameless

"Behold, it was for my peace that I had intense bitterness; but You have loved back my life from the pit of corruption and nothingness for You have cast all my sins behind Your back!" (Isa. 38:17 AMP).

14. From Stressed to Peaceful

"Peace I leave with you; my own peace I now give and bequeath to you. Not as the world gives do I give to you. Do not let your hearts be troubled, neither let them be afraid" (John 14:27 AMP).

15. From Misunderstood to Appreciated

"Yes, I have loved you with an everlasting love; therefore with loving-kindness have I drawn you and continued my faithfulness to you" (Jer. 31:3 AMP).

16. From Ambitious to Humble

"He guides the humble in what is right and teaches them his way" (Ps. 25:9 NIV).

17. From Worthless to Treasured

"For he who touches you touches the apple of his eye" (Zech. 2:8 NKJV).

18. From Compromised to Secure

"When my heart is overwhelmed, lead me to the rock that is higher than I. For thou hast been a shelter for me. . . . I will trust in the cover of thy wings" (Ps. 61:2–4 KJV).

19. From Lonely to Loved

"Do you think anyone is going to be able to drive a wedge between us and Christ's love for us? There is no way! Not trouble, not hard times, not bullying threats, not backstabbing . . . none of this fazes us because Jesus loves us" (Rom. 8:37–39 Message).

20. Transformed

"And we, who with unveiled faces all reflect the Lord's glory, are being transformed into his likeness with ever-increasing glory, which comes from the Lord" (2 Cor. 3:18 NIV).

"And so we are transfigured much like the Messiah, our lives gradually becoming brighter and more beautiful as God enters our lives and we become like him" (2 Cor. 3:18 Message).

Beware the god your mind invents, for you'll inevitably worship and become like him; however wretched, however false. Best of all, find the true God; and filling your mind with the truth of His being, you'll learn His love and treasure the life He creates. All else is confusion. All else is ultimate despair.

Jack W. Hayford, pastor and author,
Rebuilding the Real You

Before We Say Good-bye

> I am a little pencil in the hand of a writing God who is sending a love letter to the world.
>
> Mother Teresa

This project began as the result of a conversation I had with a friend who happened to mention in passing that she thought the Bible was the most boring book she had ever read and that she had come to the conclusion Jesus was a fraud.

Several months later, when she heard I was writing a book, she asked me what it was about. You can imagine my trepidation when I told her, "The book is about Jesus and the relationship he had with the women in his life."

She looked at me with an expression of utter disbelief as she blurted out, "I didn't know Jesus knew anything about women!" She continued, "Dorothy, do you really think a man who never married, had no children, no home, no job, no money and wandered the hills with twelve men could relate to my problems? The hassles I face today? You've got to be kidding!"

Her response caught me off guard. While I anticipated a less than enthusiastic reaction, her candor got me to thinking: *Can Jesus really understand the needs of a woman like me?*

Over the last few years, as I have put pen to paper, my friend's blunt but honest feedback has served as a tremendous motivator. I began to realize that if Jesus could not meet the needs of the women in his own life, how could I ever expect him to meet mine? So I studied, read, discussed, and prayed, and with time, the pages of this book began to fill with the stories of eighteen women whose lives intersected with Jesus. Out of the shadows these ladies came, and as each one opened a window into her life, I found myself drawn in. Much to my surprise, there wasn't one woman whose path had not intertwined with mine. I found connecting points—those places where we shared common experiences. And this from a group of women living long ago, yet in reality facing the identical trials and challenges I have encountered!

But I discovered more. The lack that deterred these women from becoming all they could be, turned into plenty when they met Jesus. Time with Jesus gave each woman a life like Jesus. By beholding him, these women were changed. They began to mirror the beauty their eyes beheld. Consequently, every woman underwent a miraculous transformation.

And this brings me to the culmination of these true stories that originate with the man who loved the women. Thankfully, he is still the same man who loves women today. When I started writing this book I thought I understood just how much Jesus loves each of us. I know now I didn't have a clue! It took eighteen women to begin to show me exactly how wide and deep his love is and to what lengths he will go to reveal his love to us.

What I am trying to say is that I've fallen in love with this man, Jesus, all over again. And I hope you have too. Because if you have, his love will fill the empty spots in your life and make you whole. His love will change those things about you that you may have thought were unchangeable. And his love will empower you to do things you never thought you were capable of doing.

You'll have the courage to shout from the rooftops that your "Dad" loves you just the way you are. You'll go to the ends of the earth if he asks you to because his love will give your life purpose. And you will give everything you are to this Man who has given everything he is to you.

Exactly how does this change take place? The key to your personal transformation and mine is the same key that unlocked an explosive power in the lives of the women who were Jesus's friends. Their key was a connection to Jesus, an interaction between two people. These women found that their transformation required a transaction, so they followed Jesus. They walked with him. They talked with him. And the more time they spent with Jesus, the more they reflected him.

If you want to experience a relationship that plugs you into the transformative energy of Jesus, I encourage you to take time each day to talk and walk with the man who loves you. And as part of your devotional time, I invite you to join other women in visiting www.transformationgarden.com. Transformation Garden is a quiet place designed to help women like you and me embrace the love of Jesus every day. The apostle Paul, writing to his friends in Ephesus, encouraged them to "keep their feet planted in love" (see Eph. 3:17). He said if they followed this advice, they would be able to "grasp how wide, and long and high and deep is the love of Christ" (Eph. 3:18). And then Paul gave the Ephesians a postscript—one of those "and by the way" statements. Paul wrote that this powerful love will do "far more than you could ever imagine or guess or request in your wildest dreams!" (Eph. 3:20 Message). If you would like to fill your life with this special love—come and visit Transformation Garden.

It is my prayer that the stories in this book have led you to the man who loves you like no other, the man who will wrap his arms tightly around you, hold you close, and never let you go.

Trust steadily in God, hope unswervingly, love extravagantly.
1 Corinthians 13:13 Message

Notes

"The role of the writer is not to say what we can all say, but what we are unable to say."

Anaïs Nin, *The Diary of Anaïs Nin*, Vol. 5 (1974)

Chapter One: The Broken Women

1. Jack W. Hayford, *Rebuilding the Real You* (Ventura, CA: Regal Books, 1986), 55.

Chapter Two: The Flawed Woman

1. Kathy Keay, *Laughter, Silence, and Shouting* (London: HarperCollins, 1994), 56.

Chapter Three: The Empty Woman

1. Ben Patterson, *Waiting* (Downers Grove, IL: InterVarsity Press, 1989), 65.

Chapter Four: The Rejected Woman

1. William Whiston, A.M., *The Life and Works of Flavius Josephus* (Philadelphia: John C. Winston Company, 1952), 298, 345, 363.
2. Mark Rutland, *Streams of Mercy* (Ann Arbor, MI: Servant Publications, 1999), 39–40.

Chapter Five: The Unfulfilled Woman

1. Dinesh D'Souza, *The Virtue of Prosperity* (New York: Free Press, 2000), 243.

2. Ronald Brownrigg, *Who's Who in the New Testament* (New York: Oxford University Press, Inc., 1971), 34.

Chapter Six: The Insecure Woman

1. Faith Popcorn, *Clicking* (New York: HarperCollins, 1996), 52.

Chapter Seven: The Isolated Woman

1. Martha Borth, *Sitting at His Feet* (Keene, TX: Clarion Call Books, 1985), 35.
2. Keay, *Laughter*, 147–48.

Chapter Eight: The Hungry Girl

1. Mother Teresa, *The Joy in Loving* (New York: Viking Penguin, 1997), 213.
2. Frederic and Mary Ann Brussat, *Spiritual Literacy* (New York: Scribner, 1996), 344.
3. Quoted in an article in the *New York Times* magazine, written by James Wooten.
4. Keay, *Laughter*, 36.

Chapter Nine: The Worried Woman

1. Steve Adams, *Peace in the Midst of the Storm* (New York: Pilot Publishing).

Chapter Ten: The Ignored Woman

1. Edith Deen, *All of the Women of the Bible* (New York: HarperCollins, 1955), 189.
2. Brownrigg, *New Testament*, 264.
3. E. White, *Steps to Christ* (Boise, ID: Pacific Press), 100.

Chapter Eleven: The Labeled Woman

1. Linda H. Hollies, *Jesus and Those Bodacious Women* (Cleveland: Pilgrim Press, 1998), 44.
2. Robert J. Morgan, *Then Sings My Soul* (Nashville: Thomas Nelson, 2003), 113.

Chapter Twelve: The Hopeless Woman

1. Patrick Henry, *The Ironic Christian's Companion* (New York: Riverhead Books, 1999), 118.
2. Norman Wright, *Chosen for Blessing* (Eugene, OR: Harvest House Publishers, 1992), 129.
3. Larry Dossey, MD, *The Extraordinary Healing Power of Ordinary Things* (New York: Harmony Books, 2006), 62.
4. Ibid., 64.

Chapter Fourteen: The Stressed Woman

1. Clair Cloninger, *A Place Called Simplicity* (Eugene, OR: Harvest House, 1993), 53.
2. Borth, *Sitting at His Feet*, 81.

Chapter Fifteen: The Misunderstood Woman

1. Josephus, *Against Apion*, 2.201.
2. Michael Griffiths, *The Example of Jesus* (Downers Grove, IL: InterVarsity Press), 132.
3. Joachim Jeremias, *New Testament Theology*, Volume 1, 226.

Chapter Eighteen: The Compromised Woman

1. Ann Wroe, *Pontius Pilate* (London: Jonathan Cape, 1999), 15–16.
2. Deen, *Women*, 206.
3. Jaroslav Pelikan, ed., *The World Treasury of Modern Religious Thought* (Boston: Little, Brown and Company, 1990), 463–64.

Bibliography

I learned from the age of two or three that any room in our house, at any time of day, was there to read in, or to be read to.

Eudora Welty, *Listening* (1984)

General

Bender, Sue. *Plain and Simple*. New York: Harper and Row, 1989.

Bruce, F. F. *Jesus: Lord and Savior*. Downers Grove, IL: InterVarsity Press, 1986.

Brussat, Frederic and Mary Ann. *Spiritual Literacy*. New York: Scribner, 1996.

Chittister, Joan D. *Scarred by Struggle, Transformed by Hope*. Grand Rapids: William B. Eerdmans, 2003.

———. *There Is a Season*. Maryknoll, NY: Orbis Books, 1999.

Cloninger, Clair. *A Place Called Simplicity*. Eugene, OR: Harvest House, 1993.

Cotner, June. *Comfort Prayers*. Kansas City: Andrews McMeel, 2004.

Day, Dorothy. *The Long Loneliness*. San Francisco: HarperCollins, 1952.

Foster, Richard J. and Emilie Griffin. *Spiritual Classics*. New York: Harper Collins, 2000.

Gire, Ken. *Instructive Moments with the Saviour*. Grand Rapids: Zondervan, 1992.

Griffiths, Michael. *The Example of Jesus*. Downers Grove, IL: InterVarsity, 1985.

Hayford, Jack W. *Rebuilding the Real You*. Ventura, CA: Regal, 1986.

Hays, Richard B. *The Moral Vision of the New Testament*. New York: HarperCollins, 1996.

Henry, Patrick. *The Ironic Christian's Companion*. New York: Riverhead Books, 1999.

Hollies, Linda H. *Jesus and Those Bodacious Women*. Cleveland: Pilgrim Press, 1998.

Johnson, Barry L. *Choosing Hope*. Nashville: Abingdon Press, 1988.

Keating, Thomas. *Open Mind, Open Heart*. New York: Continuum International, 2003.

Keay, Kathy. *Laughter, Silence, and Shouting*. London: HarperCollins, 1994.

Lamott, Anne. *Traveling Mercies*. New York: Pantheon Books, 1999.

L'Engle, Madeleine. *Walking on Water*. Wheaton: Harold Shaw, 1980.

Lewis, C. S. *A Year with C. S. Lewis*. New York: HarperCollins, 2003.

Lucado, Max. *He Still Moves Stones*. Waco: Word, 1993.

Miller, Keith. *Habitation of Dragons*. Waco: Word, 1970.

Palmer, Parker J. *A Hidden Wholeness*. San Francisco: Jossey-Bass, 2004.

Patterson, Ben. *Waiting*, Downers Grove, IL: InterVarsity Press, 1989.

Rutland, Mark. *Streams of Mercy*. Ann Arbor, MI: Servant Publications, 1999.

Sider, Ronald J. *Rich Christians in an Age of Hunger*. W. Publishing Group, 1997.

Smith, Paul. *Jesus, Meet Him Again for the First Time*. Gresham, OR: Vision House, 1994.

Thurman, Dr. Chris. *If Christ Were Your Counselor*. Nashville: Thomas Nelson, 1993.

White, E. *Steps to Christ*. Boise, ID: Pacific Press.

Wright, N. T. *The Challenge of Jesus*. Downers Grove, IL: Inter-Varsity Press, 1999.

Wright, Norman. *Chosen for Blessing*. Eugene, OR: Harvest House, 1992.

Yancey, Philip. *The Jesus I Never Knew*. Grand Rapids: Zondervan, 1995.

Background Historical

Brownrigg, Ronald. *Who's Who in the New Testament*. New York: Oxford University Press, 1993.

Bundesen, Lynne. *The Woman's Guide to the Bible*. New York: The Crossroad Publishing Company, 1993.

Chilton, Bruce. *Rabbi Jesus*. New York: Doubleday, 2000.

Davis, John D. *Davis Dictionary of the Bible*. Grand Rapids: Baker Books, 1972.

Deen, Edith. *All of the Women of the Bible*. New York: Harper & Row, 1955.

Del Mastro, M. L. *All the Women of the Bible*. Edison, NJ: Castle Books, 2004.

Evans, Mary J. *Women in the Bible*. Downers Grove, IL: Inter-Varsity, 1983.

Metzer, Bruce M. and Michael D. Coogan. *The Oxford Companion to the Bible*. New York: Oxford University Press, 1993.

Meyers, Carol. *Women in Scripture*. New York: Houghton Mifflin, 2000.

Myers, Bill. *Luke Examines Jesus*. Wheaton, IL: Victor Books, 1979.

Pelikan, Jaroslav. *The World Treasury of Modern Religious Thought*. Boston: Little, Brown and Company, 1990.

Selvidge, Marla J. *Daughters of Jerusalem*. Scottsdale, PA: Herald Press, 1987.

Strong, James. *The New Strong's Exhaustive Concordance of the Bible*. Nashville: Thomas Nelson, 1990.

Tenney, Merrill C. *The Zondervan Pictorial Encyclopedia of the Bible*. Grand Rapids: Zondervan, 1975.

Whiston, William. *The Life and Works of Flavius Josephus*. Philadelphia: C. Winston Company, 1952.

Young, Robert. *Young's Analytical Concordance to the Bible*. Peabody, MA: Hendrickson Publishers.

Quotations

Agel, Jerome and Walter D. Glanze, *Pearls of Wisdom*. New York: Quill, Harper & Row, 1987.

Cook, John. *The Book of Positive Quotations*. Minneapolis: Fairview Press, 1993.

Gallagher, B. J. *Witty Words from Wise Women*. Kansas City: Andrews McMeel, 2001.

Guiley, Rosemary Ellen. *The Quotable Saint*. New York: Checkmark Books, 2002.

Maggio, Rosalie. *The New Beacon Book of Quotations by Women*. Boston: Beacon Press, 1996.

Tripp, Rhoda Thomas. *The International Thesaurus of Quotations*. New York: Harper & Row, 1970.

A Note from Dorothy

If you wish to contact me with questions and comments, or if you just want to say "Hi," I can be reached by email at: dorothy@whenawomanmeetsJesus.com or dorothy@transformationgarden.com
or by calling
1-888-397-4348
or write:
Dorothy Valcárcel
When a Woman Meets Jesus
15802 N. Cave Creek Road
Suite 2
Phoenix, AZ 85032

For information on Transformation Garden log on to: www.transformationgarden.com.

Dorothy Valcárcel has a twenty-five-year career working with charitable organizations worldwide. Her experiences have taken her into ghettos, orphanages, domestic abuse shelters, and food kitchens. The insight she gained, along with her own personal struggle to overcome challenging disabilities sustained in a life-threatening accident, are the catalyst for Transformation Garden—a website designed to encourage women in their walk with Jesus. Dorothy's daily devotionals are featured on Crosswalk.com.